1971

SEXUALITY AND MORAL RESPONSIBILITY

SEXUALITY AND
MORAL RESPONSIBILITY

BY ROBERT P. O'NEIL

AND

MICHAEL A. DONOVAN

Foreword by Gregory Baum

CORPUS BOOKS

Washington / Cleveland

CORPUS PUBLICATIONS

EDITORIAL OFFICE:
1330 Massachusetts Ave., N.W.
Washington, D.C. 20005

SALES & DISTRIBUTION:
2231 West 110th Street
Cleveland, Ohio 44102

Library of Congress Catalog Card Number: 68-18713
FIRST PRINTING 1968
Printed in the United States of America

FOREWORD

THIS STUDY OF SEXUAL MORALITY is an attempt to bridge the traditional approach to moral theology and the achievements of the social sciences. This is a courageous undertaking. Few Catholic theologians have attempted to do this. The authors of this book rightly insist that theological reflection is in need of dialogue with psychology and sociology. In the past, theologians have been in dialogue with philosophy. Since for them theology was reflection on doctrine, they readily acknowledged the need for philosophical tools in analyzing and synthesizing ideas. But if theology has to do, not so much with ideas as with the presence of God to human life, or saved humanity, then the exercise of theology demands dialogue with the social sciences.

The authors of this book acknowledge the change that has taken place in the self-understanding of man. With Vatican II they acknowledge the evolution occurring in man's experience of himself. "The human race has passed from a rather static concept of reality to a more dynamic, evolutionary one" (*The Church in the Modern World,* n. 5). The moralist, in particular, is greatly impressed by the enormous widening of the area of personal responsibility. Many aspects of human life, about which the older generation could shrug their shoulders and remain indifferent, have moved into the area of personal responsibility. Types of behavior at one time regarded as good and commendable are being questioned today. In a culture—to give an example—in which people cannot vote or exert other influence on the political and social policies of their country, it was moral for Christians to remain ignorant of worldly affairs. Ardent Christians of the past sometimes withdrew altogether from contact with the world. In our day, however, when it is possible to vote and influence the policies of a country through public opinion, a Christian may no longer withdraw from the political aspect of life. What was good at one time has, in a new situation, become sinful.

Modern man has also discovered that the area of personal responsibility in sexuality is wider than he had supposed. Older generations tended to look upon sexuality simply as a biological fact and they were willing to submit their lives to the laws determined by the biological finality of sex. Today sexuality is understood as a wider human reality. What we do not know at this time is the total role of sexuality in God's saving plan for the human race. How are we being transformed through the sexual dimension of our personalities? While we do not know all the answers, we must remain open to man's evolving self-understanding and attempt to discern what personal responsibility means in this new context.

The present book is a bridge. It lays the foundation in traditional neo-scholastic terms and then adds new considerations drawn from the social sciences. This leads to modifications of the traditional views which are quite startling. The authors reject an act-centred moral theology: morality for them is the responsible orientation toward growth and reconciliation. In their discussion of sin they reject the idea that a single act can, by itself, produce man's separation from God; they acknowledge, on the contrary, that many minor infidelities can create a state of mind in which man is totally alienated from the divine summons to new life. These principles enable the authors to exclude the category of "mortal" sin from the moral evaluation of sexual acts. The authors differ from traditional Catholic moral theology in their evaluation of sexual fantasies and feelings and the role of masturbation in growing up. While the authors defend the traditional position on premarital sexual intercourse, they interpret this norm in the context of the growing love and intimacy through which man and woman move to the stable union of married life.

The present book is a bridge. This is also its weakness. Some readers may ask themselves why the authors did not acknowledge the new self-understanding of man from the beginning and set out to find a new starting point for the moral evaluation of human life. The attempt to bridge two distinct approaches inevitably leads to a certain eclecticism. The authors realize this difficulty. But they feel that in the present situation of Catholic thought a book of this kind is necessary, not indeed as the last word on the moral issue but as a passage toward a more profound understanding of sexual morality.

Some readers may be disturbed by the apparently untheological character of the book. The Good News of salvation is hardly ever mentioned. The authors occasionally speak of man's relationship to God but his relationship is hardly clarified. Some readers may feel that there has taken place an uncritical borrowing from the social sciences and that the moral tone of the book is reminiscent of naturalism. Such an impression, however, would be deceptive.

The theology of the present study is largely implicit in what the authors mean by human growth and reconciliation. The Good News of salvation is packed into their anthropology. The authors still seem to employ the method of traditional, neo-scholastic moral theology which took as its doctrinal basis a few principles derived from revelation, without permitting itself to be confronted by the Word of God at every step. For the authors of the present study the doctrinal basis of their moral reflections is God's redemptive involvement in the growth and reconciliation of mankind, a position endorsed by Vatican II. For the authors man's humanization is not a purely natural process determined by man's own resources. They acknowledge in faith that man's humanization is a process in which the divine summons to new life is ever present. "We witness the birth of a new humanism, one in which man is defined primarily in terms of his responsibility towards his brethren and toward history" (*The Church in the Modern World*, n. 54). God has involved himself in man's making of man.

GREGORY BAUM

PREFACE

THE BASIC NOTION that has guided our work is our strong conviction that a viable morality must be solidly grounded in the established principles of the behavioral sciences. Theoretically speaking, few people would disagree. Yet we are struck by the many areas of moral teaching and sacramental-pastoral practice which, in spite of rapid strides in theological renewal, still exhibit serious conflicts.

We are afraid of the danger of misunderstanding here. When we speak of good psychology we are not invoking the current "fashions" in science (such attempts at integration have been only too disastrous in the past) nor are we referring to relatively untested hypotheses or mere theories. We are talking about substantive, empirically established facts and essential assumptions which are in the mainstream of thinking in clinical, developmental, and social psychology. A "viable" morality, similarly, refers to perennially valid principles of Christian theology which, when applied to the constantly changing circumstances of life, furnish a guide to conduct that is both conceptually and experimentally valid. In our present attempt at outlining a synthesis in a few moral areas we therefore feel quite justified in by-passing a great accumulation of casuistry and established prejudices that have hindered moral theology for so long.

Our aim in this book is threefold. First we wish to present some fundamental changes in viewpoint necessary to such a restructured morality. Much of this is hardly original (such men as Monden, Schillebeeckx and Schoonenberg, to name a few, would defend a similar orientation), but we think that our interdisciplinary approach establishes a broader basis for further thinking than can be obtained from solely theological research. Second, we wish to offer an approach, an integrated theological-psychological point of view, to be used by others in the analysis of similar problems. Third, we wish to recommend some specific changes that can form a partial solution to specific problems.

The content of this book begins with a developmental consideration of moral responsibility during childhood in Chapter One. Chapter Two attempts a theoretical integration of the facts of psychology and dogmatic theology as they bear on the nature of sin. Chapter Three is a bridge between the theoretical issues and some specific problems, focusing upon the importance of sexuality in all aspects of personal functioning. Each of the last three chapters discusses the moral and psychological dimensions of one important sexual-moral problem.

The changes we propose may in some cases be radical departures, not from the roots of Christian tradition, but from questionable interpretations translated into moral teachings. These interpretations have arisen in part from a lack of communication with the sciences, in part from an attitude of paternalistic overprotection that has persisted from a time when it may have been needed, and in part from a response by theologians to the faithful's search for secure direction and authoritative, specific answers.

The material in this book is directed to three groups. In terms of personal interest, it is for college students and young adults who are in the process of developing adult standards of morality; of integrating, often with great difficulty, previously unquestioned doctrine with new intellectual and experiential insights, often a part of the so-called "crisis of faith." In terms of policy, it is aimed at pastors and educators who are responsible for initiating and implementing change. And it is for parents, who are the key influence in the religious, moral, and sexual education of the person.

We wish to express our appreciation to *Insight* and the Herald Press for permission to use material originally published by them as part of Chapter One.

CONTENTS

SEXUALITY AND MORAL RESPONSIBILITY

THE MAGIC YEARS

FOR MANY YEARS, the *Catholic Digest* and other similar periodicals could be counted on for humorous anecdotes about children's confessions. An eight-year-old boy confesses that he has committed adultery ten times, because he has used the outdoors rather than a urinal; a nine-year-old girl confesses a bad habit of detraction and addition; three ten-year-olds confess genocide for stepping on ants, and another miscreant sinned with his eyes and ears, because the eyes crossed while the ears wiggled *in the classroom.* Seriously, though, examples can be multiplied by any parish priest who regularly is subjected to the sing-song, memorized recitals of hundreds of regimented penitents from grade school. Some reflection makes it clear that these common anecdotes are far more tragic than comic. These children are expressing not knowledge of and sorrow for an offense against God, but their confusion and a desire to please. Unfortunately, the confusion and attitudes of childhood often persist into adulthood with little change.

If the child cannot understand abstract concepts and relationships, it is clear that he cannot distinguish between mortal and venial sin, or between sin and fault. How, then, is morality to be presented to the preadolescent child? The answer may be to exclude the idea of sin altogether. An even more serious question involves the teaching of such highly abstract concepts as God, the Trinity, and the soul. Questioning of the child will elicit definitions of these concepts in keeping with his instruction. But beneath this verbal facade, what does the average child really think God is, and what are his attitudes toward him? God, in the minds of all too many children, is a patriarchal, punitive figure; the Trinity is inextricably intertwined with a three-leaf clover or triangle, and the soul is a sort of white heart that can be blackened by sin and bleached by confession.

A thorough evaluation of moral and religious training in the light of psychological facts must result in a profound desire to change and improve the present system. Changes thus far, although constructive, have been limited to modifications of the prevailing system. It may be that a basic rethinking is necessary before the products of eight or twelve years of religious education equal the products of fifteen to twenty-five weeks of adult instruction classes.

In moral and religious dimensions, as in all other aspects of personality development, the child is indeed father of the man. That is, mature moral living is based upon sound, developmentally congruent early experiences and training. If the child is exposed to attitudes or values that he cannot understand or is led to believe in a sin-oriented morality, as an adult he will have to deal with the long range consequences of this training.

We feel that current catechetical and pastoral practice, as it relates to children under the age of twelve to fourteen, is theologically and psychologically harmful. It leads to distortions in the concept-values of such religiously basic ideas as God, sin, salvation, and freedom. Any attempt to integrate psychological findings with traditional moral concepts forces one to the conclusion that children are incapable of anything morally culpable until the age of twelve or fourteen. That is, although they can do wrong, they cannot commit even venial sin. This may seem unreal, but the logical conclusion is inescapable. We believe that an almost total restructuring of moral teaching is necessary in order to achieve a theologically and psychologically valid approach to human moral development.

On a question as important as the determination of a threshold for moral responsibility, theology must be at least as cautious as the behavioral sciences. For example, in seeking to determine the threshold at which sound or light can barely be perceived, the accepted rule is that the stimulus must evoke a response in at least 50 per cent of the trials at a given level. A second relevant consideration may be borrowed from the psychological testing of age-related abilities. Age-related abilities are those the performance or mastery of which increases with age, such as the comprehension of ideas or complex motor skills. The rule in this case is that at least 50 per cent of the children at a given age level must respond correctly in order to consider the test question appropriate to that age level. In addition, the percentage of children passing an item must increase during successive age levels. A final consideration is borrowed from statistics. To be relatively certain that research results are not due to chance, the rule used is the "5 per cent level of confidence," i.e., confidence that the event could have occurred by chance only five times out of one hundred.

These considerations are introduced to illustrate some of the controls used by scientists to prevent subjective bias, a small sample, or other errors from influencing conclusions. The more important the conclusions, the more rigid are the controls and insistence upon proof. But in the all-important area of determining the lower age boundary for moral responsibility, moralists have relied upon tradition and assumption, rather than demanding proof that this capacity is indeed present at the assumed age level. There is ample evidence to be presented later that this capacity is not operational at this time.

It must be made clear from the start that preadolescent children are unquestionably capable of doing wrong; they can commit acts which are forbidden, omit those which are required, know what they are doing, expect punishment, and feel guilt, shame, and remorse. *This does not, however, constitute mature moral consciousness.* Rather, the child's understanding of right and wrong has a ceiling imposed by the level of cognitive development, that is, capacity to understand, maturity of judgment, and life experiences. Even if we use the current definitions of moral theology, children below the age of 12-14 are incapable of either mortal or venial sin. A brief review of the psychological facts and theological reasoning will support this assertion.

PSYCHOLOGICAL RESEARCH FINDINGS:

INTELLECTUAL DEVELOPMENT

Our first consideration will be the empirical evidence pertaining to the development of the child's intellectual capabilities at different age levels. This development is sequential; that is, each stage builds upon the preceding one. In the area of cognitive development, the Swiss psychologist Jean Piaget has made probably the greatest contributions.[1] His work spans more than forty years and has resulted in over twenty-five books and a hundred and fifty articles. In his research Piaget amassed a great deal of evidence which led to his conclusion that formal operational thinking (the full and perfect use of reason) does not appear until about eleven or twelve years of age at the earliest.

Formal thought is defined by two criteria: the ability to carry out a mental experiment, i.e., hypothetical reasoning from assumptions or definitions rather than from concrete reality, such as syllogistic or deductive reasoning, and an ordering and awareness of the thought operations, such as retaining definitions. Formal thought includes such examples as drawing conclusions from logical propositions, reasoning from instances to a general rule, and the capacity to evaluate one's own thinking critically.

Prior to this age, children's thought processes are generally *egocentric, syncretic, non-logical, concrete* and *non-relational.* Children see the world with themselves as the center. They do not admit diversity of opinion or equally correct alternative explanations. They fail to distinguish between cause and coincidence, between substantial and superficial, and are unable to understand abstract relationships. Most children, for example, believe that traffic laws are more fundamental than the Bill of Rights, that grandparents were never children, and that the wish is equivalent to the deed. Of the above terms "syncretic" needs further elaboration. The syncretic character of preadolescent thinking is defined by Piaget as:

a type of thinking which absorbs reality into global, undifferentiated schemas; the individual contents of the assimilated reality interpenetrate and fuse with one another, anything being joined to or combined with anything else simply by virtue of common membership in the loosely bounded schematic potpourri.[2]

Examples are the confusion of whole and part, and of cause and effect. The syncretic thinking of childhood reveals itself in a child's belief, for instance, that words have meaning apart from reality or that misfortune is a punishment for misdeeds.

Piaget found that as late as eleven or twelve years of age, syncretic thought persists and hinders the comprehension of concepts. The younger the child, the more concrete the thinking. Commenting on the problem of grasping two-way relationships, Piaget stated: "A simple relationship like that of brother still presented insurmountable difficulties to the child of 9-10."[3] Werner also described the structure of thought in preadolescent children as diffuse, concrete, and characterized by one-way relationships. The higher level of thought, that which is articulated, abstract, and relational, he placed at about thirteen to fifteen years of age.[4]

Discussing the age range of 7-11 years, Piaget's "subperiod of concrete operations," John H. Flavell stated:

> The older child seems to have at his command a coherent and integrated cognitive *system* with which he organizes and manipulates the world around him. Much more than his younger counterpart, he gives the decided impression of possessing a solid cognitive bedrock, something flexible and plastic and yet consistent and enduring, with which he can structure the present in terms of the past without undue strain or dislocation.[5]

He went on to describe the many infra-logical, concrete-operational mental tasks of which the preadolescent child is capable, such as complex mathematical operations. However, he specified several crucial limitations: "Concrete operations are concrete, relatively speaking; their structure and organizing activity is oriented toward concrete things and events in the present. . . . The starting point is always the real, not the potential."[6]

Moving to the period of eleven to fifteen years of age, Piaget's stage of formal operations, Flavell stated:

> The most important general property of formal operational thought, the one from which Piaget derives all others, concerns the *real* versus the *possible*. . . . It amounts to a fundamental reorientation toward cognitive problems. . . . formal thinking is above all *propositional thinking*. In general Piaget finds that contrary-to-fact "what if" suppositions tend to be foreign to the thought of middle childhood. . . . No longer exclusively preoccupied with the sober business of trying to stabilize and organize just what comes directly through the senses, the adolescent has, through this new orientation, the potentiality of imagining all that might be there.[7]

I. E. Sigel, in a review of 135 theoretical and empirical articles on the attainment of concepts, stated:

> During the period of approximately seven to eleven years of age our reasoning processes *begin to appear logcal* (italics ours). In children seven to nine, concepts are still limited in inclusiveness, that is, not all instances of a category are included. The employment of categorical labels still has elements of concrete aspects.[8]

In another section, he concluded: "Induction of concepts into an inadequately mature cognitive organization can result in a hollow core of concept acquisition."[9] In other words, the premature training of a child to memorize concepts before he can integrate them can result in apparent understanding. For example, children can memorize the Gettysburg Address and Act of Contrition; yet questioning reveals incredible ignorance and confusion over their meaning. Later, however, when the capacity to comprehend is present, the person is not able to rethink and analyze the concepts, and they remain at an immature, poorly understood level. Many adults, for example, have not abandoned ideas such as the apple in the Garden of Eden or that creation took place in six days.

M. Laurendeau and A. Pinard reported on their study of cognitive development, using 250 boys and 250 girls from various intellectual and socio-economic levels between 4 and 12. One of their conclusions was: "The child's mode of thinking does not reach the operational level in all content areas simultaneously but is rather subject to horizontal time lags whereby the same intellectual structures are successively applied to different contents."[10] They also concluded that most research data supports Werner's admonition that the child's observed facility in reproducing or producing concepts does not necessarily mean that the underlying intellectual process is accurately reflected.

The fact is that even young children can retain and reproduce concepts which they have been taught without any shadow of understanding or integration of these ideas. A child of six or seven can parrot a definition of gravity or repeat a paragraph on the nature of angels, but cannot, and should not be expected to, criticize or explain his statements. This must not be confused with an underlying intellectual process that does understand the terms and the reasoning behind them.

The content of intelligence tests for children and adolescents shows a shift in emphasis from concrete to abstract, from motor to conceptual items at about eleven to thirteen years of age. The two most widely used individual intelligence tests for children, the Stanford-Binet Intelligence Scale and the Wechsler Intelligence Scale for Children (WISC), differentiate concrete from conceptual responses and score them differently. The vocabulary subtests of both scales, those most highly correlated with overall I.Q., contain words of increasing abstractness.

In discussing the research findings, theoretical articles, and tests cited above, the authors at no point consider abstract, conceptual, relational thinking possible *in a consistent and sustained way* before eleven to thirteen years of age. The italicized phrase is necessary since certain ideas and relationships may be learned by some children at an earlier age. However, these isolated instances must be regarded as precursors rather than as a sampling of sustained ability.

Reinforcing Sigel's conclusion concerning the premature induction of concepts and Werner's admonition concerning overt concept reproduction not being an accurate reflection of the underlying intellectual process is this quotation from Bruner's *Study of Thinking*: "In short, the attainment of a concept has about it something of a quantal character. It is as if the mastery of a conceptual distinction were able to mask the preconceptual memory of the things now distinguished."[11] A roughly comparable example is the inability of an adult to truly understand the child's confusion about adult sexuality, or a practiced swimmer to recall his fright and lack of coordination before he learned to swim.

One may argue at this point that the exceptional or precocious child, because of his accelerated mental development, should be capable of mature moral acts and judgments at a significantly earlier age than the average. If this were true, it would nevertheless apply to only a small fraction of the population. In fact, however, the results of research on moral development, political thinking, and the development of autonomy of judgment, to be discussed next, reveal that even high I.Q. cannot overcome the developmental obstacle and that age, maturation, and experience are far more determining than is intelligence in the development of the capacity for moral acts.

MORAL DEVELOPMENT

Gesell and his co-workers, in their developmental studies, have discussed the development of conscience and ethics:

> The ten year-old is just beginning to distinguish between right and wrong. . . . Characteristically, ten is concretely specific. . . . He is somewhat naively susceptible to ethical teaching, and over-reacts to it with what resembles a self-righteous attitude. In these various patterns of behavior, Ten displays transparently the persistence of childhood characteristics—the concreteness of his "moral" orientation and the simplicity of dependence shown toward his mother. With adolescence there will be reorientations, but in general they will be gradual rather than precipitous, and they will be governed by the growth of social intelligence and the new attitudes toward his peers.[12]

Piaget, in carrying out his research on cognitive development, pioneered research in the development of moral judgment. One of his most significant findings was the discovery of age-related changes in six aspects of the development of moral judgement.

These have been verified by other researchers and were described by L. Kohlberg as follows:

1. *Intentionality in judgment.* Young children tend to judge an act as bad mainly in terms of its actual consequences, whereas older children judge in terms of the intent to do harm.

2. *Relativism in judgment.* The young child views an act as either totally right or totally wrong, and thinks everyone views it the same way. The older child is aware of possible diversity in views of right and wrong.

3. *Independence of sanction.* The young child says an act is bad because it will elicit punishment; the older child says an act is bad because it violates a rule, does harm to others, etc.

4. *Use of reciprocity.* Younger children do not use reciprocity as a reason for consideration of others. By age eleven to thirteen, most children can clearly judge in terms of ideal reciprocity, in terms of putting oneself in the place of someone in a different position.

5. *Use of punishment as restitution and reform.* Younger children advocate severe painful punishment after stories of misdeeds; older children increasingly favor milder punishment leading to restitution and to reform of the culprit.

6. *Naturalistic views of misfortune.* Younger children tend to view accidents and misfortunes occurring after misdeeds as punishments willed by God. Older children do not confuse natural misfortune with punishment.

In the same paper, which is a review of 120 theoretical and experimental articles, Kohlberg evaluated these findings as follows:

These six aspects of moral judgment have proved to define genuine dimensions of development in the grammar school years. They increase regularly with age, regardless of the child's nationality in western cultures, his social class, his religion, or the particular stories or situations about which the child is questioned.[13]

Some other relevant conclusions that Kohlberg drew from the research are that intellectual development is an important condition for the development of moral thought and that judgment does not appear to become "moral" until early adolescence, while "morality" of conduct appears to develop early. Finally, he stated: "The research findings on the slow age development of moral judgment, ego strength, and self-criticism suggest the wisdom of a gradualistic view of the child as morally accountable."[14]

In another review of more than 140 theoretical and experimental articles, Kohlberg concluded that moral internalization and judgment relate closely to cognitive development of moral concepts. This means that until the person has attained sufficient maturity of thought and understanding to comprehend fully the concepts of morality, he is unable to integrate the values into a coherent, workable system for himself. In addition, the evidence suggests strongly that what may be called "conscience" develops quite late. Intelligence is not highly related to more mature judgment; whereas, chronological age is related highly, strengthening the conclusion that high I.Q. alone cannot overcome the developmental obstacle.[15] That is, more than intelligence is necessary for mature moral judgment. The child must have a sufficient amount of experience in living and maturing.

Independent and converging evidence on the age-related nature of cognitive and moral development comes from research on political thinking. The relevance of this evidence is apparent when one considers the similarity in many respects between moral and political concepts. Both are based upon relational thinking—one's relation to God and neighbor and one's relation to the state and to the community. In both cases, mature thinking demands the overcoming of egocentrism and concreteness, and the use of concepts such as reciprocity, the future, and the community.

J. Adelson and R. P. O'Neil reported the results of a study using a lengthy, free interview with 120 boys and girls from ten to seventeen years of age. The subjects were led through many of the traditional problems of political philosophy, such as the function of government, the purpose of law, and individual versus society's rights. The problems were presented by means of abstract questions, situations demanding concrete solutions, and dilemma questions in which the subject was forced to defend his position against counter-arguments. The results revealed statistically significant progressive age differences in the attainment of political concepts. Certain concepts, such as the community as a structure and the continuity of the community, were simply not available to even the bright children at ten or eleven years of age. By fourteen years of age, however, the majority of children demonstrated a truly conceptual grasp of political concepts.

The fifth grade group viewed government and the law much as they do parents and parental commands. Decisions are not to be questioned; law is a necessary restrictive control of potentially bad or destructive impulses, and the more laws the better. The younger children in the sample favored rigid, harsh law enforcement and stiff punishment for infractions. The older children were more flexible, willing to modify laws, and tended to suggest remedies rather than punishment.

In certain respects, the fifth and seventh grade groups were set apart from the ninth and twelfth grade groups. Both younger groups had difficulty grasping the concept of the continuity of the community; neither group could transcend the assumptions or alternatives in a question; neither group had developed a feeling for the rights of the community; both groups had a parental idea of government, and neither had a clear idea of the relationship between government function and governmental structure.[16]

These findings, in a different content area, correspond exactly with the results of research in cognitive and moral development. The younger children's thinking is essentially concrete, authoritarian, non-relational, and egocentric. The attainment of concepts is dependent more upon chronological age and experience in living than upon intelligence, religion, or social class.

The results of Kohlberg's research in moral thinking and O'Neil's research in political thinking also point to the age-related development of autonomy of judgment, corroborating Piaget's conclusions. Kohlberg found a high correlation between a child's resistance to an adult interviewer's pressure to change his judgment and his level of moral development. O'Neil found that autonomy of judgment was almost absent at ten years of age and not really well established at twelve years. Not until fourteen years of age was it clear that a significant proportion of children was capable of questioning and understanding the assumptions and premises of questions or able to reject presented alternatives in favor of their own ideas. Older children were also much more able to resist counter-arguments in dilemma questions and to defend their positions. Children up to fourteen years of age often changed their position twice on a question when presented with an argument supporting the opposite point of view.[17] Clearly, the first position that these children chose did not stem from a grasp of principles nor from propositional thinking.

CONCLUSIONS FROM PSYCHOLOGICAL RESEARCH

From the research results presented in the preceding section, several conclusions may be drawn:

1. The "age of reason," defined in terms of cognitive development sufficient to enable the child to comprehend concepts, grasp relationships, and understand distinctions, occurs at the onset of adolescence, that is, between eleven and thirteen years of age in almost all children.

2. Autonomy of judgment sufficient to make responsible moral decisions manifests itself somewhat later, probably between twelve and fourteen years of age.

3. Prior to this developmental level, children's thinking is egocentric, syncretic, non-logical, concrete, and non-relational. Children's judgments are heteronomous, rigid, authoritarian, and inconsistent.

4. The development of thinking and judgment in moral matters follows a developmental sequence determined primarily by cognitive development and age-related experience.

5. Although manifestations of mature thinking and judgment may occur prior to the onset of adolescence, these are precursors of developing capacities, not evidence of consistent and sustained ability.

We have outlined the psychological capacity of the child in the area of morality. To integrate this with the teaching of the Church, it is necessary to review the position currently held by moralists on the capacity for moral acts in children.

At a recent pastoral institute the Redemptorist moral theologian and Vatican Council *peritus*, Bernard Häring, remarked concerning the subject of mortal sin and children's confessions:

> The most rigid opinion might say that after ten years of age they [children] are capable of mortal sin. *I doubt if a child of eleven or twelve years can commit a mortal sin.* They must know what a mortal sin is—that the merciful and just God punishes with a terrible sentence for all eternity. It is not in a moment that a child or man decides his destiny, it is through the whole of life. Every exaggeration harms the sacrament of mercy.[18]

This opinion seems to contain obvious truth to all who deal with children's consciences, whether as teachers, parents, or confessors. Yet it is unusual to see such a remark in print. The fact is that while almost everyone admits that little children of seven or eight years do not and indeed cannot commit subjectively mortal sins, no theoretical proof for this belief has been put forth in theological or catechetical journals.

CANON LAW AND THE AGE OF REASON

Canon 12 states that all who have attained the use of reason are bound to observe the ecclesiastical law unless the law itself expressly states the contrary. Canon 88 defines that those who have attained their *seventh year of age are presumed to have reached the age of reason.* We insert the italics because certain theologians have said that canon law does not presume that seven years is the age of reason; yet the Penal Code of Church law expressly includes children over the age of seven, binding them, in at least one case, to the severest of penalties—automatic excommunication.[19] But there is no question that the law presumes that children of seven or eight years of age are capable of mortal sin and therefore ought to go to confession.

The use of the arbitrary age of seven years to mark the beginning of the power of rational evaluation of motives and goals (the "age of reason" or the "age of discretion") derives from the jurisprudential norms embodied in the Code of Civil Law of the Byzantine Emperor Justinian I, promulgated in 529 A.D.[20] This norm of Roman civil law was incorporated into the general law of the Church. It is tragically unfortunate that the ancients lacked insight into what we call today developmental psychology. The child was considered in practice "homuncular," a miniature adult. Once having attained the age of reason he was liable to incur all the sanctions of adult law. This attitude persisted up to relatively modern times. Even in supposedly enlightened England of the eighteenth century, children were hanged by common law for petty theft.

Canon law, like all human law, is strongly conditioned by such factors as time and culture. Torture was once legal as a means of extracting confessions, even in Church law.[21] This was old Roman Law, and the rediscovery of Roman Law—"divinely wise"—in the Middle Ages had a profound influence upon the formulation of Canon Law. The jurisprudential norm in question here (the determination of the age of reason at seven years) was never critically examined; it was simply accepted.

By a complex historical process Canon Law strongly influenced the moral theology taught in seminaries. This moral theology is not the moral theology of the great thirteenth century Scholastics, but rather is a tool of confessors, designed to enable them to ascertain the minimum standards requisite for maintaining the state of grace.

Although the term "state of grace" is a Catholic term, it can, for the purposes of this book, be extended to include similar concepts from other theological points of view, such as friendship with God or a close relationship with God. Current moral theology draws heavily upon legal concepts. By and large, it is a post-Tridentine development. This theology in turn profoundly affected preaching and teaching, notably catechetical indoctrination. And it forms the commonly accepted guide of pastors in their day-to-day administration of the sacraments, particularly Penance.

It is obvious that Canon Law assumes children over the age of seven years to be capable of subjectively serious moral evil (in Catholic terms, mortal sin). It is likewise obvious that this assumption is seconded by contemporary pastoral practices, such as requiring children to confess before receiving first Holy Communion and teaching second grade children the theological distinction between mortal and venial sin. For those who may doubt the validity of this assertion, any current parochial school or C.C.D. religion texts, except for a few notable recent exceptions, will convey far more eloquently than our words the obsession with sin, punishment, and guilt that pervades the moral and religious education of Catholic children. Although the idea that children of seven or eight cannot commit serious sin is fortunately emphasized in current texts, there is, nevertheless, a depressing amount of material devoted to sin, offending God, and showing him that we are sorry. For example, in one second-grade text[22] a particular lesson aims "to develop in the child a real hatred of sin because sin offends God and hurts us" (p. 24). The next lesson tells the teacher "We should train the children to examine their consciences frequently. . . . It is a very good means of avoiding serious sin" (p. 26). "After recognizing a fault or sin, the child should immediately turn to God, ask His pardon, and beg His mercy" (p. 26). "God is very much displeased when His children commit sin" (p. 29). "When we sin we offend Someone who loves us very much. We offend God. And when we tell God our Father that we are sorry, we want to think only of Him and how we have offended Him" (p. 32).

Another second-grade text[23] contains an illustrative guide for an examination of conscience: "Have I failed to love the Heavenly Father by: (1) Failing to turn to God, my Father, and to pray to Him, especially in the morning and at night? (2) Misbehaving in Church, . . . If we have not been faithful to God our Father we will pray: *God, my Father, I am sorry for having offended You. Forgive me*" (p. 122).

It is unfortunate that the creativity of religious educators is restricted by the idea that children can commit sin. The positive attitude toward God that is currently being taught is all but negated by the child's preoccupation with sin and sorrow for having offended this confusedly perceived Being.

The gross anomaly is apparent to any thinking person: while no court in the modern world would even indict (much less condemn to capital punishment or life imprisonment) a child under the age of ten, we have been teaching that an all-good, all-just and all-merciful God and Father (Who loves and understands them more than their parents could hope to) will condemn them for an act that they may, and probably will, commit! We need not labor the point. Current religious pedagogy and pastoral practice in this area is based upon a jurisprudential norm totally out of harmony with modern jurisprudence, not to mention psychological fact.

THEOLOGICAL REQUIREMENTS FOR MORTAL SIN

Mortal sin, in Catholic theology, is the greatest personal disaster that can befall a man in his relationship with God. It consists in the deliberate rejection of Almighty God conceived of as one's "final end" and the turning to some created good in preference to the love of God. Häring lists the three essential elements involved in mortal sin:

> First, an object strictly commanded or strictly prohibited, in actuality or at least in the estimation of the agent. This is often called "grave or serious matter;" secondly, clear awareness of conscience regarding the command, the seriousness of the law, often called full advertence; thirdly, the free decision of the will, often called full consent of the will. Should any of these elements be missing entirely or substantially, there is no mortal sin committed; at most the offense is venial.[24]

Mortal sin is any serious violation of the law of God. Children of all ages are at least certainly *capable* of objectively criminal acts. For example, a child can steal large amounts of money, inflict grave injuries on another, or deliberately lie and put someone in a very difficult position. Our question, however, is whether children are capable of *subjective* mortal sin—actually incurring the guilt and punishment due to deliberate estrangement from God. In every mortal sin there is implied a *fundamental* choice, a deeply personal orientation which gives direction, significance, and value to the whole of man's life. In the case of a sincere person, this life-attitude is a moral one, i.e., the will of God above all things. If an individual performs actions which are inconsistent with this basic orientation but which do not destroy his fundamental choice to do God's will, such actions do not separate him from God. This is a venial sin.[25]

Since sin is fundamentally an act of the will, the subjective element in mortal sin, that is, volition proceeding from deliberation, is the most important factor. The culpability of an action will depend upon the free will and deliberation of the agent. Häring, giving the common teaching of Catholic theologians on this point, says:

> If the knowledge of the importance of the act or the degree of actual advertence to its gravity is essentially lessened, the freedom of the act itself is correspondingly diminished, *for the freedom of the act does not go beyond the bounds of the moral consciousness*; however, it may be that the freedom of the act may not be total and complete, even though there is clear knowledge and full advertence of the mind.[26]

Sufficient intellectual advertence and full consent of the will, essential constituents of mortal sin, must be the exercise of a mature moral consciousness. Mortal sin, as traditionally defined, is a concrete, specific act of the will involving a practical judgment; but this judgment (and the will act which follows upon it) is necessarily based on certain abstract concepts and judgments of the intellect. St. Thomas says that the ultimate judgment concerning acts belongs to the higher reason, as does the consent. Judgments concerning lesser matters or preliminaries may be made by the lower reason, but always subject to the judgment of the higher reason. The "higher reason" St. Thomas speaks of is the intellect itself, the immaterial faculty of logical, reflective, analytical, and critical thinking. The intellect judges ultimately the morality of an act by critically examining the act in the light of principles and goals it already possesses.[27] In the case of mortal sin, the intellect must judge the act in relation to the universal principle governing the whole of one's existence: God perceived (at least confusedly) as one's highest good.

The intellectual thought process leading to mortal sin, then, is:

1. *abstract*: the values and concepts involved are wholly non-sensible (God, grace, eternal punishment, life-goal);
2. *relational*: the essence of mortal sin is the rupture of the personal bond between the individual and God;
3. *critical*: not merely cognitive, but profoundly *evaluative* thinking is necessary in every choice involving a basic orientation of personal life.

Is this type of thinking possible in children prior to the onset of adolescence? The evidence presented demonstrates that it is not. Inasmuch as the psychological evidence also bears on the question of venial sin prior to adolescence, we will first discuss the traditional currently accepted theology of venial sin.

VENIAL SIN

The entire Thomist school of theology, along with many theologians of other schools, agrees that *no sin, even the slightest venial sin, is subjectively possible until the possibility of mortal sin is present.*[28] This opinion is intrinsically at least strongly probable in theology. Until now it could not be certain, since scientific developmental psychology is a relatively new field, and the recent practice of the Church in hearing children's confessions at an early age apparently contradicts this opinion. But the practice of the Church in this regard has never been subjected to critical evaluation in the light of modern psychology. It has been *assumed* that children at the age of seven could commit mortal sin, hence they were *presumed* to have committed venial sin. But the great scholastics were wise enough to refrain from attempting to define the precise age at which this might occur. Venial sin, as mortal sin, was tied to the age of reason established by Justinian.

What is venial sin? Without going into all the subtleties controverted by theologians, all agree that it can be defined only in its relation to mortal sin or to the ultimate end of man. Mortal sin is the conscious or deliberate rejection of God explicitly or implicitly perceived as one's final end. It is the turning to some created good in such a way that one seeks one's final end in the creature, thereby ceasing to love God above all things and severing one's friendship with him. Venial sin, by contrast, does not sever one's friendship with God. The will loves a created good inordinately, but the "deordination" is not such as to destroy one's basic orientation toward God. When St. Thomas teaches that venial sin is called "sin" only analogously, he means that the full and perfect notion of sin is found only in what we know as mortal sin; venial sin bears some resemblance (analogy) to it.[29]

Considering venial sin in its relation to mortal sin, as we must, it is morally certain in theology that venial sin is a true moral evil, a disorder in the pursuit of one's final end, a deflection but not a complete turning away from the true good of human life. St. Thomas teaches in this connection that mortal sin is concerned with the end directly, while venial sin concerns the means to the end. Venial sin, therefore, can be formally sinful only if it is seen consciously as something inconsistent with the pursuit of one's final happiness.

But a means cannot be formally a means unless the end has once been consciously and deliberately chosen, although it may be so materially. This means that until a goal has been chosen, no behavior can be labeled a means toward that goal. However, behavior that becomes a means when a goal is chosen can, prior to this, be a means to another goal or several different goals. "The first act of the free will is rightly said to be of a special order and to be necessarily grave, at least objectively, because it bears on the end and not on the means, since the means cannot be chosen until the end has been willed."[30] For example, if I choose to drive from Detroit to Chicago, every mile that I drive west is a means to that end, bringing me closer to Chicago. If I have no intention of going to Chicago, but drive west to visit friends, every mile that I drive does in fact bring me closer to Chicago; but it would be absurd for someone to judge that I was going to Chicago merely because I was headed west.

Similarly, children are capable of actions which are, materially, greater or lesser violations of the moral law, such as stealing, vandalism or lying. Furthermore, they can consciously and deliberately will these evil acts. Such acts are radically oriented toward future subjective sin and predispose the child to commit real sin later in life. That is why children must be trained in right moral behavior from their earliest years. However, the goodness or badness of these acts flows from the child's concrete relationships with parents, teachers, siblings, and playmates, as well as his impulsiveness and immaturity of controls, rather than from moral decision. They can be only materially sinful.

St. Thomas firmly teaches that children cannot commit venial sin until they possess sufficient use of reason to commit mortal sin. It is not an isolated opinion, but is part of his formal doctrine on the nature of sin and man's final end. In his *Summa*, St. Thomas asks "whether venial sin can be in anyone with original sin alone and without mortal sin." He states in the body of the article:

> I answer that it is impossible for venial sin to be in anyone with original sin alone, and without mortal sin. The reason for this is because before a man comes to the age of discretion, the lack of years hinders the use of reason and excuses him from mortal sin, wherefore, much more does it excuse him from venial sin, if he does anything which is such generically. But when he begins to have the use of reason he is not entirely excused from the guilt of either venial or mortal sin. Now the first thing that occurs to a man to think about then, is to deliberate about himself. And if he then direct himself to the due end he will, by means of grace, receive the remission of original sin; whereas if he does not then direct himself to the due end, as far as he is capable of discretion at that particular age, he will sin mortally, through not doing that which is in his power to do. Accordingly therefore, there cannot be venial sin in him without mortal, until afterwards all sin shall have been remitted to him through grace.[31]

In his commentary on this article, McCabe says:

> The discussion of the impossibility of venial sin being present in one who has only original sin leads St. Thomas to an analysis of thought-life in man. *Before one arrives at the age of discernment, when he can see the distinction between good and evil, or what is called the use of reason, he cannot commit a sin of any kind, and cannot have venial sin in his soul* (italics ours). When a man begins to use his reason, the first thing he does is to begin to think about himself, and

to give his life purpose. If he turns to God at this time, he receives the remission of . . . sin through the Baptism of Desire. If he does not turn to God, he commits a mortal sin. . . . Therefore, venial sin is possible only after the remission of original sin or the commission of the first mortal sin.[32]

The term "age of reason" has always been understood in theology and canon law as that age at which true moral acts are possible, the age at which the distinction between right and wrong can be discerned and when mortal sin can be committed.[33] The idea that a person could have sufficient use of reason for a true moral act and be at the same time incapable of mortal sin is an anomaly, a contradiction in terms. To act morally is to be capable of judging a particular act evaluatively in terms of moral principle. This demands a full and perfect use of reason. Commenting on St. Thomas' use of the term "use of reason" in Article Six, F.C.R. Billuart says:

> By the term "use of reason" we do not mean any use of reason, but a full and perfect use of reason which suffices for deliberation regarding serious matters, for discerning moral good and evil, for choosing a goal in life, and so forth. But this perfect use of reason is not acquired all at once, but only gradually, and in a step-by-step process. . . . How much time is required for this, whether a week, a month, a year or more, cannot be defined.[34]

Häring, commenting upon the wellsprings of moral activity, says: "When we refer to acts as the subject of moral value, it is obvious that we are referring to the properly human acts which have their root in the spiritual center of the person, in insight and freedom."[35] Again, Billuart says that every moral act (and therefore venial sin) implies at least the faculty or power of perfect use of reason. Of course he admits that once perfect use of reason is attained, imperfect reasoning is enough for venial sin, but not before that:

> In order to sin venially from surprise or indeliberation . . . it is necessary that one have the power of perfect deliberation and control over each of his acts individually, although not over all of them;

but a child who has not attained the perfect use of reason which is required for mortal sin does not have this power.[36]

Furthermore, the very distinction between true moral good and moral evil cannot be grasped until complete and perfect use of reason is attained: "To arrive at the full and perfect use of reason is to be able to discern moral good from evil, and thus in that very instant to see the connection, through synderesis, with the natural law dictating that moral good must be sought and evil avoided."[37] Moral good, the *bonum honestum*, is not formally a concrete reality. It is a good of the whole man, a good which is, or contributes to, man's ultimate end. To apprehend this good (or its opposite, moral evil) requires abstract, relational, critically evaluative thinking. Just as a child cannot commit mortal sin because he is incapable of this kind of deliberation; so too, he cannot commit venial sin, because such sin, even though slight, nevertheless requires a real moral choice, based on real moral judgment. This demands the capacity for full and perfect reasoning. Speaking of venial sin which is venial because of small matter, Billuart states:

It seems certain that there can be no use of reason sufficient for venial sin which is not likewise sufficient for mortal sin; for it is much easier to ascertain what is seriously sinful than what is only slightly so. Thus, anyone who realizes that an idle word, a jocose lie, a small theft is evil would, *a fortiori*, know that perjury, homicide, and grand larceny is evil.[38]

Cardinal Cajetan, in his Commentary on the *Summa*, is apodictic on this point:

[St. Thomas says] that much more does [the lack of the use of reason which excuses a child from mortal sin] excuse him from venial sin. The reason for this is that the lesser is included in the greater. For it stands to reason that, all other things on the part of the subject being equal, mortal and venial sin *ex genere* are related as the greater to the lesser. . . . Therefore, an act committed by a child, even though it be objectively grave, is not imputed to him if there is lack of sufficient liberty; *a fortiori* such a lack of liberty suffices to render a less serious act non-imputable to him.[39]

Further in his commentary, Cajetan goes on to show how, if we say that children can commit venial sin though not mortal sin because of their imperfect act of reasoning, this is contradictory. For a sin which is venial because of the imperfection of the act implies necessarily the radical capacity to perform perfect acts:

> Sin which is venial by reason of the imperfection of the act presupposes sufficient freedom for the commission of mortal sin; for it presupposes that it can be prevented by an act of free will. So, to a child who is excused from mortal sin because of a lack of freedom, no movement whatever toward either mortal or venial sin is imputed, on account of the lack of perfect liberty with which to anticipate, prevent, or control these movements.[40]

Summing up the opinions of theologians before him, Billuart says:

> These are the solutions of Thomists commonly, after Cajetan, with which the Salmanticenses and Gonet also agree, presuming that there is some imperfect freedom in the child before the perfect use of reason is attained. This [imperfect freedom] does not produce acts which are morally indifferent, but only physically so; for in order to perform free acts which are morally indifferent there must be *an understanding of the harmony or disharmony between one's acts and the rules of morality, which is not had unless there be perfect use of reason* (italics ours).[41]

Finally, Canon Law itself makes a black-and-white distinction concerning moral responsibility. Canon 88, No. 3 states that having attained the age of seven years, a child is presumed capable of full use of reason and therefore of mortal sin; before age seven, a child is considered *non sui compos*, capable of no sin whatever.

It is clear from the preceding sections that moral acts as traditionally viewed demand a level of intellectual development capable of making conceptual, evaluative distinctions consistently. It is also clear that the capacity for thinking in terms of two-way relationships must be present in more than a rudimentary manner. In addition to cognitive maturity, there must be relative autonomy of judgment. The psychological research findings presented demonstrate that conceptual thinking and autonomy of judgment suffi-

cient for true moral acts *as currently defined* are not present consistently in the average child before twelve or thirteen years of age.
The psychological evidence is incontrovertible. Many persons today
accept the fact that children cannot commit serious sin. The aim in
presenting the psychological research has been in part to provide
the empirical foundation for that fact. Far more importantly, we
wish to evaluate the true moral potential of the child at different
levels of development.

GENERAL CONCLUSION

Integrating this theological evidence with the conclusions previously stated from the psychological research, a further general conclusion must be drawn. *Lacking the ability to make true moral
judgments, preadolescent children are incapable of committing
mortal sin. Since there cannot be venial sin without the possibility
of mortal sin, they are, therefore, incapable of committing any sin.
Hence, there is no matter for the valid administration of the Sacrament of Penance.*

This last point may seem too strong for most persons to accept.
However, it has been demonstrated that children are incapable of
subjective mortal sin. They cannot make the kind of decision, nor
commit the kinds of acts for which God would condemn them.
Because this mature moral consciousness must be present before a
child can commit venial sin, no sin is possible. Therefore, the
preadolescent child is pre-moral, maturationally incapable of sin
and, conversely, incapable of truly virtuous or meritorious acts.

Most persons will disagree with this conclusion. The current
problem is the result of several causes. The primary cause appears
to be the view held for several centuries that children were miniature adults, that certain capacities were attained very early in one
spurt of development and then levelled off into adult functioning. A
second cause was the preoccupation with the morality of the
overt act and the legalistic narrowing of consciousness to the specific of behavior, rather than intention. Because children can and
do commit acts which externally duplicate adult sins, the inevitable

conclusion was drawn. A third cause that persists is the view that moral responsibility is a black-and-white, all-or-none kind of thing.

We hope to integrate the insights of doctrinal teaching with the truth of psychological knowledge and to begin to build a realistic developmental morality from this fusion. The entire area of pre-adult moral responsibility and education needs restructuring. It is true that children are capable of controlling their behavior or of consciously doing wrong, of adhering to principles or of deliberately violating them. It is also true that children, prior to adolescence, are incapable of making a fundamental moral choice which can condemn them to eternal punishment. Their inability to commit mortal sin and, by classical moral definition, venial sin, must be integrated with the scientific and common sense evidence that children are able to do good and avoid evil or to ignore the good and do wrong.

Just as a child is led step by step into an understanding of mathematics and grammar, the facts indicate that he can be led into an understanding of moral responsibility. A child is told that there are certain things which adults can do of which he is incapable. A child cannot commit himself to serious evil for the same kind of reason that he cannot run a 4-minute mile or pole-vault 17 feet—he is maturationally incapable. His maturational level limits his athletic feats, his skill with tools, and his understanding of concepts. The child understands this, just as he understands that practice and the right kind of training now will help his chances of doing things well when he is able. The same holds true for moral responsibility. True, long-range evil can be committed only by older children and adults; whereas, he is only able to commit short-range faults. However, the child can appreciate the necessity of preparing and training in moral habits.

DEVELOPMENTAL LEVELS OF MORALITY

The essence of childhood morality is obedience. The child is subject to the rules of parents, teachers, and others in authority over him.

He is not allowed nor expected to make free decisions. This is not limited to moral matters, but holds true in every area of his life: school attendance, medical examinations, curfew, spending money, and so forth. Legally, a child cannot even be culpably negligent of his own life, as attested to by ordinances concerning swimming pools, traffic laws, etc. Only in adolescence, and then little by little, is the child encouraged to exercise some self-direction in any vital areas.

We have the research findings from various areas of psychology that the development of the individual in all aspects of his functioning is a long, gradual process. Certain functions must follow a developmental sequence of stages; that is, the child must walk before he can run and perceive objects before he can comprehend concepts. This is the case in the development of moral judgment and responsibility. Because of the influence of cognitive maturation, age, and life experiences, there are levels in children's lives at which they are ready to understand and act upon moral teaching. The following is an attempt to articulate these levels and their corresponding "moral readiness."

At the preschool level, it is obvious that we are not dealing with any personal responsibility on the part of the child. Moral culpability can hardly be imputed when toilet training is in some cases not fully established. The child at this age is not, however, incapable of learning. On the contrary, he is learning at a primitive and extremely powerful level. Preverbal learning, as evidenced by research, is the foundation of what will later become character and moral habits. The vehicles of this type of learning and personality formation are primarily the child's identification with the parents and parental reinforcement, through praise and punishment, of developing traits and qualities in the child. The child identifies with and takes in as his own those values, ideals, and norms which the parents act upon and exhibit. If discipline is consistent, he will also learn that certain actions and objects are forbidden, while others are likely to result in praise.

The long lasting effects of early childhood training are not in dispute. The strength of these early habits lies in the fact that they are not formally taught with words or charts, but are taken in without awareness. Formally instructed lessons can be resisted, but this kind of training cannot. The responsibility, therefore, for the formation of correct habits and attitudes is upon the parents and is very grave. There is no sharing this responsibility.

MIDDLE CHILDHOOD

From school entrance until about nine years of age, the period of middle childhood, the child makes some significant advances in moral development. An essential step is taken when the self-critical ability of the child reaches a level of relative stability. During these middle years of childhood, this aspect of ego functioning is apt to fluctuate wildly, from an almost total lack of self-criticism to a fever of self-condemnation. The stabilization of this function depends primarily upon the emotional climate concerning moral responsibility and discipline in the home. Equally as powerful on another level is the formal training in religion and morality. Formal teaching which emphasizes a punitive attitude, demands mature responsibility, or assumes an unrealistically high level of self-control can contribute to severe conflicts between a rigid conscience and an ineffective self-control system.[42]

Toward the end of this developmental level, the die is more or less cast in terms of an enduring set of emotionally powerful standards of right and wrong. By this time, the child is relatively advanced in the capacity to judge his actions (and those of others) against these values. If the code is developmentally realistic, he has *at best* an immature and inconsistent self-critical function, strongly influenced by changing feelings and the attitudes of others. If, on the other hand, the values have not been integrated at appropriate times or in manageable doses, he is subject to excessive guilt and shame over behavior and feelings which are perfectly normal. The important point to bear in mind about the child's developing capacity for self-criticism is that no matter how stable the environment or how supportive his important adults are, this is a multidetermined attitude that cannot be more mature and rational than the personality from which it springs.

A second relevant advance during these years is the beginning of concept formation discussed earlier from a research point of view. The child's verbal facility and memory enable him to deal with a variety of concepts, but from a basically concrete point of view. Mathematics, science, and grammar can be presented at this age level in an intelligible manner. Religious and moral concepts that are of a low level of abstraction or easily related to his daily life and interests stand a good chance of integration also.

Concept formation is closely tied to the development of social attitudes, such as group identification and reaction to group pressure and the ethics of social behavior that result. Value concepts of honesty, fairness, generosity, and sharing can be abstractly formulated and grasped by the child if he can see their concrete application to his real-life situations. Specific instances of telling the painful truth, sharing a prized toy, or controlling anger can be labeled by parents as good qualities and reinforced by praise.

What do these relatively vague statements regarding middle childhood tell us about the subjective moral potential of children at this age? If they cannot make a vital decision or commit themselves to the long-range consequence of mature moral responsibility, just what is the limit of moral culpability during these years?

We must begin our explanation with yet another developmental fact, that is, that children can know about many things before they can do them or even experientially understand them. Sexual functioning is the best illustration of this point. Morally, children can be taught the difference between long-range evil and short-range faults. They can understand that shortcomings now can result in severe problems later. Therefore a child must be open to developing and sustaining those values, attitudes, and habits which will form the core of his moral orientation later. He is "responsible" for his preparation. This demands an orientation, an attitude of receptivity to the commands and counsel of parents and those who stand *in loco parentis.*

We must emphasize that the "responsibility" we speak of is not fully *moral,* because moral responsibility demands an understanding of the relationship between behavior and the ultimate purpose of human life. It is concrete and act-specific. A child does not act on moral principle, but on the specific rules of "grown-ups." Acts of disobedience are a part of growing up, to be handled within the family. In order to develop those qualities which will be of long range value, the child must submit himself to the teaching of adults. This attitude will be reflected in the child's judgment of his own acts. Those that coincide with the orientation will be judged good; those that oppose it will be judged bad. This judgment in turn can be reinforced by parents and teachers. Parents have a powerful tool in rewards and punishment for keeping the orientation in the right direction. Discipline, properly understood (not punishment), is the mechanism of reinforcement for the orientation of the child.

What if the child does not live up to this responsibility? Can he sin in any theological sense? We must answer this question with some vagueness. Certainly there are some sanctions applicable before the child reaches adolescence. But do these sanctions have to be moral? It would be more in keeping with what we know of traditional morality and psychology to say that the ultimate responsibility lies with the parents at this age. If the sanctions were strictly moral, the child would be bound to follow his own conscience, not the advice or commands of parents. Parents, teachers, and others are still responsible at this time to see that the child gradually internalizes their values and acts accordingly. They must guide and counsel, reward and punish to make sure that the child is developing those habits and attitudes which, when he attains the age of moral resposibility, will have him oriented toward God. The adults are responsible to God for the child. The child is only responsible to those who teach him.

The difference in moral development between the pre-school years and the period of middle childhood is, for the child, small. It cannot be otherwise. Children cannot be expected to grasp the full implications of moral habits and training. They may understand the words, but cannot possibly grasp the idea of life-goal, final end, or commitment to God. Their planning is still short range, subject to whimsical changes. We do not expect them to make less important decisions independently. They cannot choose their subjects in school, contract minor debts, or be punished for felonies. Why, then, are moralists and educators so eager to have children at this age subject to moral culpability for even "venial" sins?

It would seem sensible to consider children of this age moral as well as legal minors. We should regard their moral behavior much as we regard their financial, educational, or athletic behavior—as a period of trial and error learning, a time of preparation and training. Their responsibility is to learn and practice, to heed advice and to be subject to the judgment of their parents.

It does not distort the concept of God to say that he would reward striving to do good and ignore the lapse from good at this age. Meritorious acts or states would be situations or patterns of reacting in which the child chose what he knew to be right despite the temptation to do the opposite. This is a precursor of mature ego functioning and good moral behavior. At this age, the choice to follow impulse and pursue gratification, even though it has been judged wrong, is a symptom of childhood immaturity, not a sign of rejection of God or an inconsistency with some consciously chosen aim in life.

LATE CHILDHOOD

Late childhood begins at about nine years of age and lasts until twelve or thirteen, the beginning of adolescence. By the end of this period the child has moved into the level of formal abstract thinking. This is the single most important morally relevant development during these years. It means that the young adolescent can begin to perceive and comprehend God as final end and ultimate good. He can appreciate a personal relationship with God and can begin to solidify it on his own without the mediation of parents. During the years from nine to thirteen or so, the child is in a phase of moral transition. He is moving from responsibility to parents toward responsibility to God. The child before age ten or so has no freedom in a uniquely human way to make moral choices. The child from ten to thirteen gradually progresses to the point at which he can make critical, evaluative, consistent moral judgments based on ab-

stract relational thinking. In the course of this cognitive development, attitudes toward God, responsibility, good and evil mature
also. This means that more and more frequently, the preadolescent
is aware of a reciprocal relationship with God that is not mediated
by parents, one that is personal. The concept of God during this
time becomes more mature, and at times the long range implications of the concept "God" and the relationship between God and
person are comprehensible.

We must emphasize that these flashes of insight and the con-
comitant feeling of responsibility are *inconsistent.* They occur
within a personality structure in which all aspects of development
are irregular. The preadolescent child, therefore, is not morally
responsible in a long-range, consistent, and sustained manner. He
is, however, in the process of becoming responsible to God for his
judgments in matters that he perceives as relevant to his relationship with God. These matters are still of short-range implication to
the child. They do not involve a mature moral decision.

The critical point to be made regarding the entire period of life
prior to the onset of adolescence is that the child is maturationally
incapable of long-range evil. Second, wrong or bad decisions and
actions are not *moral,* but are a result of immature ego functions.
As such, they must be treated as any other symptom of immaturity,
not assigned to a realm of concepts and attitudes unintelligible to
the child and certainly injurious to his developing relationship with
God.

NOTES TO CHAPTER ONE

1. See for example: J. Piaget, *The Language and Thought of the
Child* (New York: Harcourt, Brace, 1926); *Judgment and Reasoning in
the Child* (New York: Harcourt, Brace, 1928); *The Moral Judgment of
the Child* (London: Kegan Paul, 1932).

2. J. H. Flavell, *The Developmental Psychology of Jean Piaget* (New
York: Van Nostrand, 1963), 273.

3. J. Piaget, *Judgment and Reasoning in the Child* (New York: Harcourt, Brace, 1928), 96.

4. H. Werner, *Comparative Psychology of Mental Development* (New York: International Universities Press, 1948; rev. ed.).

5. Flavell, *op. cit.*, 165.

6. *Ibid.*, 203.

7. *Ibid.*, 205.

8. I. E. Sigel, "The Attainment of Concepts," in *Review of Child Development Research*, M. L. Hoffman and L. W. Hoffman, eds. (New York: Russell Sage Foundation, 1964), I, 214.

9. Sigel, *op. cit.*, 241.

10. M. Laurendeau and A. Pinard, *Causal Thinking in the Child* (New York: International Universities Press, 1962), 251.

11. J. Bruner, Jacqueline Goodnow, and G. Austin, *A Study of Thinking* (New York: Wiley, 1956), 50.

12. A. Gesell, Frances Ilg, and Louise Ames, *Youth: The Years from Ten to Sixteen* (New York: Harper, 1956), 465.

13. L. Kohlberg, "Development of Moral Character and Moral Ideology," in *Review of Child Development Research, op. cit.*, 398.

14. *Ibid.*, 426.

15. L. Kohlberg, "Moral Development and Identification," in *Sixty-second Yearbook of the National Society for the Study of Education* (Chicago: University of Chicago Press, 1963), 322.

16. J. Adelson and R. P. O'Neil, "Growth of Political Ideas in Adolescence: The Sense of Community," *Journal of Personality and Social Psychology*, IV (1966), 295-306.

17. *Ibid.*, 305.

18. Midwestern Institute of Pastoral Theology, August, 1964, Detroit, Michigan.

19. See *Catholic Encyclopedia*, I, 209.

20. *Code of Justinian*, Book 18, VI, 30.

21. Bull of Innocent IV, *Ad extirpanda*, 1252, cited in P. H. Hughes, *A History of the Church* (New York: Sheed and Ward, 1952), 410-411.

22. Mother Mary V. Pfeiffer, *The Body of Christ* (New York: Sadlier, 1966), Teacher's Guide.

23. Sister M. Johnice and Sister M. Elizabeth, *Come, Lord Jesus*, Book 2 (Boston: Allyn and Bacon, 1967), Guidebook.

24. B. Häring, *The Law of Christ* (Westminster, Md.: Newman Press, 1964), 352.

25. P. Riga, *Sin and Penance* (Milwaukee: Bruce, 1962), 44.

26. Häring, *op. cit.*, 353.

27. *Summa Theologiae*, I-II, Q. 74, art. 7, trans. by Fathers of the English Dominican Province (New York: Benziger, 1947).

28. F. C. R. Billuart, *Summa Sancti Thomae*, II (Paris: 1876), 571.

29. St. Thomas Aquinas, *Quaestiones disputatae de malo*, Q. 7, art. 2, ad. 10.

30. E. Mersch, *Theology of the Mystical Body* (St. Louis: Herder, 1951), 267.

31. St. Thomas, *Summa*, I-II, Q. 89, a. 6; *Sent. dist.* XLII, Q. 1, a. 5; *De Veritate*, Q. 24, a. 12, ad. 2; *De malo*, Q. 5, a. 2, ad. 8; Q. 7, a. 10, ad. 8.

32. Benziger, English ed., *Summa of St. Thomas Aquinas*, III, 3251.

33. H. Noldin and A. Schmidt, *Summa Theologiae Moralis*, I: *De principiis*, 140-141.

34. Billuart, *op. cit.*, 567.

35. Häring, *op. cit.*, 189.

36. Billuart, *op. cit.*, 570.

37. *Ibid.*, 67.

38. *Ibid.*, 569.

39. Sancti Thomae Aquinatis, *Omnia opera*, editio Leonis XIII, VII, Commentary of Cardinal Cajetan, 147.

40. *Ibid.*

41. Billuart, *op. cit.*, 571.

42. M. L. Hoffman, "Child-rearing Practices and Moral Development: Generalizations from Empirical Research," *Child Development*, XXXIV (1963), 295-318.

CHAPTER TWO

SIN AS ORIENTATION

AT THE HEART of basic moral teaching is the concept of sin. Catholic dogmatic theology has admirably defined the metaphysics of personal sin as the turning away from God implicit in the choice of some created good as one's final end. Scripture shows us the malice of sin as the breach of fidelity in the sinner's love for the God "who has first loved us." The analysis of the mentality of the sinner, his personal guilt, and the plethora of elements that constitute serious sin is the domain of moral theology. A tragedy of centuries' standing is the severe disproportion between the concept of serious sin as understood in dogmatic and biblical theology and the concept employed in common pastoral practice. This unfortunate hiatus is largely the fault of post-tridentine nominalistic casuistry, with law and jurisprudence as the framework for its principles and conclusions.

We propose a redefinition of the concept of serious sin in terms of orientation rather than of act. The theological and psychological evidence to be presented warrants the assertion that there is no single action that a person could perform which would be sufficient for condemnation. Conversely, a multitude of minor actions or omissions, none of which is serious but each of which weakens the moral orientation, is sufficient to bring about a state of grave moral evil.

In law, of course, great emphasis necessarily must be placed on the legality of acts, for only externalized acts can be dealt with by law. Morality is different. Morality embraces the total complex of the human person; such strictly interior realities as judgments, de-liberation, drive, and emotion are critically important. Classical moral theology has always recognized this. In the textbook treatises on the impediments to freedom, allowance is made for internal and external obstacles to the exercise of free will: ignorance and passion, force and fear, and so forth. The questionable assumption in all this, however, is the notion that man is perfectly free in his acts until the contrary is proved, that is, unless there is reason to suppose that an obstacle has been placed to modify, restrict, or destroy liberty. The rigorous application of this assumption has led, particularly in our times, to the widespread conviction that moral theology is unreal—that it too blithely dismisses the existential complexities of human life and views man as a composite of discrete acts constantly vacillating between grave sin and grace, heaven and hell.

The factor most responsible for the present state of confusion in moral thinking and practice is the traditional focus upon the act as the vehicle of morality. By focusing upon the act, grave injury has been done to the concepts of God, justice and mercy, and the nature of man. Symptomatic of this preoccupation with the morality of act are the textbooks, from the primary grade through graduate moral theology, which in one form or another ask the question: "Is this act a grave sin?"

ATTRIBUTES OF AN ACT

Before moving into research concerned with act and its relation to the other dimensions of personality, there are some qualities of an act to be discussed. First, an overt act is generally of short duration. Most morally relevant acts occur in a few moments. Some are prolonged, but a specific act generally takes place in a very short period of time. Second, most acts are under some form of social constraint. For example, social learning keeps us from performing acts that range from assault to spitting on the floor. This pressure is not identical with conscience or moral principle, but operates as a powerful control. Third, most human acts are, to a greater or lesser

degree, psychologically determined. That is, because we are the
kind of persons we have become, there are many acts we perform
or omit as a result of habit, attitude, inhibition, guilt, shame, or
embarrassment. These qualities of an act will be discussed in
greater detail in the next section.

A further qualification of an act is necessitated by the fact that
most actions do not demand, indeed rarely can arouse, full cognitive or intellectual engagement. That is, rarely does a person fully
think through the reasons for and against an act, including all the
long range implications and the effects upon others. Most decisions
about acts are made on the basis of habit, not reason. For example,
people don't take time out of the day to fully weigh decisions such
as what to have for dinner, how to discipline the children, or when
to make a dental appointment. Most decisions follow the path of
least resistance, habit, and emotion. Moral decisions are made the
same way. The degree of emotional involvement in an act is critical
in any attempt to assess responsibility, for emotional and intellectual control over an act vary inversely; that is, the more emotional
arousal, the less intellectual control there will be.

Finally, the principles of continuity, regularity, and consistency
of personality functioning lead to an assertion that will be discussed
later: *any act is generally only as valid an indication of moral life-
orientation as any other randomly selected, consciously aware, and
morally relevant sample of behavior.*

The contradictions between religious teaching and pastoral
practice, fundamental principles and current interpretations, theological assumptions and psychological facts dictate a total restructuring of basic theological thinking, teaching, and practice.

Moral theology is perhaps the latest of the theological sciences
to be affected by the profound renewal transforming the face of the
Church today. It almost had to be this way. Moral theology, being
the "practical" part of the theological sciences, must assume as its
principles the truths and insights already established in the areas of
scripture studies, history of doctrine, and the rest. The vast changes
that have established the "New Theology" must be assimilated into
the theoretical structure of moral theology also, if the pastoral
mission of the Church is to have any real effect on the life of

modern man. If moral theology is going to speak the truth about man in his attitudinal and behavioral relationships toward himself and others in the light of the Gospel, *moral theology must begin by speaking the truth about man himself*. Just as the sciences of linguistics, literary criticism, and archeology have done so much to vitalize modern scripture studies, so moral theology must be enlightened by the discoveries of anthropology, sociology, and psychology. Only in this way can a renewed theology of human behavior attempt to be *true to life*.

It cannot be emphasized too strongly that when we speak of the behavioral sciences as necessary complements to any study of morality, we are firmly opposed to faddism. Not every sociological study or psychological theory will do to support the principles of something so crucially important or far-reaching in its consequences for Christian development as moral theology. Only conclusions tested by years of experience or principles which are accepted as constituting the very foundation of these sciences can be safely used.

One of the greatest trials of a high school or college chaplain is the frequency with which students will approach the sacrament of penance (often more than twice a week) to confess "mortal sins" committed against purity. In this regard, John T. Noonan mentions an order promulgated by the Superior General of the Jesuits in 1612 forbidding them, under pain of excommunication, to teach that there is any smallness of matter in sexual sins. That is, all sexual sins involve matter of mortal sin, never venial.[1] It forces the question: If every one of the other ten commandments can be broken in a non-grievous way, why not the sixth? Few Catholic high school or college students have this obvious fact explained to them. Many young people are sufficiently docile or scrupulous to put up with this implicit contradiction between day-to-day moral difficulties and doctrinal teaching. Others are more logical and consistent; they abandon the religious practices along with the contradictions, or they develop a more consistent personal morality without the contradictions.

Were it not so tragic, one could almost be amused by the

absurd lack of correlation between "official Church teaching" on the one hand and evaluations of personal moral behavior on the other. Not infrequently, a person who is sufficiently perspicacious and sensitive to this dichotomy gives up his religion.

INDIVIDUAL FREEDOM

It is a phenomenon of our century that so many lines of contemporary thought—religious, literary, socio-psychological—converge upon the central core of man's being, his freedom. One result of this self-scrutiny has been a serious tension between the "perfectly free," autonomous element in man and the fully determined, unconscious, irrational, and impulsive components of human behavior. An important consequence of this tension is the emergence of a concept of human freedom that is no longer simplistic. Rejecting the static, either-or absolutism of past moral thinking, modern thought has embarked upon an enormously complicated attempt to assess man himself as he tries to live out a life of mature responsibility amid all the vicissitudes of his concrete existence.

Man is certainly free. *But he is free in a specifically human way.* It is wholly beyond the scope of this book to enter into a lengthy philosophical analysis of freedom. "All theory is against the freedom of the will," said Samuel Johnson, "all experience for it." Both empirically and as taught by our faith as Christians, we believe in human freedom and responsibility. What we are attempting to assess and apply is the *mode* of human freedom. *It seems apparent that a man does not—indeed cannot—commit himself totally to a given orientation, goal, or course of action in any single, specific act.* Man is not capable of self-actualization all at once, but only gradually. Only throughout a more or less lengthy course of action (even, conceivably, only in a lifetime) can a man freely express what is his ultimate and innermost self in a truly definitive way. The commitment to marriage, for instance, is not made at the moment of the wedding. It begins early in the dating relationship, is deepened when the couple begins to go steady, and is strengthened throughout the engagement. The process of committing oneself also extends well into the marriage itself. The same holds true for commitment to the religious life or to any profession.

Retaining the classical terminology, Schoonenberg distinguishes between "mortal" sin and the "sin unto death"—and "sin unto death" alone is the confirmation in evil that condemns man to hell. For Piet Schoonenberg, mortal sin is indeed something that destroys the loving relationship between the sinner and God, but, taken in itself, it remains revocable. The ultimate hardening of the sinner in his attitude of rebellion against God is the result of many serious sins, each of which actualizes more and more his will's determination to egoism.[2]

Perhaps Schoonenberg might have done better justice to his research and fine theological reasoning by abandoning the terms "mortal" and "venial" sin altogether. It is possible to understand these terms properly, but given the abuse they have suffered so long, it is far better to scrap them. We prefer to describe the state of personal serious moral evil as a cluster of personality variables which militate against an individual's loving God and others in any meaningful way. For example, when we speak of a person's political or economic orientation, we are referring not to purely intellectual, emotional, or social dimensions, but to the composite of all these factors. Such must be the case also in serious moral evil. A man cannot be compartmentalized: "A good tree cannot bear bad fruit, nor a bad tree bear good fruit."

For example, consider the case of an elderly lady who attends daily Mass, belongs to the Third Order, and has made ninety times nine First Fridays. Close to death, but quite in control of her mind, she decides that her relatives have treated her shabbily. She upbraids them unmercifully and changes her will, giving all her money to charity in order to avenge her bad treatment. Can she by this action negate seventy-five years of saintly conduct? Ridiculous example, one is tempted to say. Yet this very type of case was being debated in moral theology classes just a few years ago.

Consider a student who has been to a late party on Saturday night. On Sunday morning he awakens sober but pained. In cold blood, he decides to miss Mass, violating a precept that he feels is gravely binding. Does this relatively dispassionate decision obviate the preceding meritorious years? Not so ridiculous, one must admit, but he *had* been drinking and was not fully awake, so the decision is not that critical.

Let us push the issue a bit further. A young family man in a better-than-average income bracket has been living at the outer limits of his income. The marriage has been turbulent recently; their anniversary is tomorrow, and he is broke. An impressive gift and an evening on the town would help to smooth things over. Fully aware of the gravity of his action, he steals $100 from petty cash, not intending to pay it back. If he were to die on the way home, unrepentant, would he be condemned? Most people would have to say yes. But our question is: to what extent does each of the above acts truly represent the person's relationship with God?

A state of grave moral evil is an ego-syntonic orientation; that is, it has a comfortable fit with the person's self-concept. One does not have to go to the parable of the pharisee and the publican to illustrate this point. Racial prejudice, graft, income-tax cheating, and expense-account padding are examples of faults that easily turn into patterns that are assimilated into the structure of the self little by little. At first, there may be the necessity for some rationalization and justification. But as the twinges of conscience or self-reproach grow weaker, the behavior is no longer seen as bad or evil, but as necessary, competitively justified, or even as evidence of sound judgment. By the time a vice is firmly entrenched, it is no longer perceived as alien to the self, but is rationalized and defended as is any other habit or attitude that forms part of the self-concept.

Pride, the point of the parable of the pharisee and the publican, is the greatest of personal grave sins in traditional theology, yet is rarely confessed. The reason is obvious: serious pride is ego-syntonic and therefore cannot psychologically be confessed, because it is not perceived as wrong. Sermons concerned with the morality of behavior for the most part concentrate on faults and shortcomings which are alien to the idea that most persons have of themselves. This has the unfortunate effect of reinforcing their present habits and attitudes. Sermons on sexuality are almost invariably aimed at adolescents and single young adults, while the topic of sexuality in marriage, with a much larger target audience, is generally ignored.

Is there any single action that a person could perform which would be sufficient to warrant condemnation? On first thought, the answer is yes. After all, isn't mortal sin, by definition, a gravely forbidden act knowingly and willingly performed? Deeper analysis compels us to take the position that this is psychologically impossible. To clarify our point that man's freedom to commit serious moral evil worthy of eternal punishment can only be the final fruit of a series, a course of individual "mortal" sins, needs amplification. A proper understanding of human freedom is critical to any discussion of grave moral evil. Most modern thinkers agree that freedom is essentially a *process of self-actualization*. This conception of freedom is not wholly foreign to classical theology, although it has been restricted and, to some extent, distorted by the case-method moral theology of the past several hundred years. Although not essential to our argument, it might be useful to summarize the classical philosophy of freedom developed by St. Thomas. Here, as elsewhere, what sometimes seems to be innovation proves to be rediscovery.

In the metaphysics of Thomistic scholasticism, freedom is a highly analogous concept. St. Thomas always views it in the light of those examplars of perfect freedom which are found in God, angels, and man before the fall. What is the common element in all these species of freedom? There must be something in man's freedom found also in God and pure spirits, else we could not use the same word in all three cases. God, of course, in this philosophical framework, is utterly unchangeable. Divine freedom cannot be any sort of choosing to act or not to act, or the choice between two different goods (in the sense that such acts imply change). And because God is infinite goodness, there is no possibility of his choosing between good and evil. Freedom in God is identical with the divine essence itself. It is the infinite love of God eternally in possession of its object.

The eminent freedom we ascribe to God, then, can only be understood as infinite self-actualization not as a process, but as a kind of dynamism having neither a goal in something nor from something else which, literally, is constitutive of the divine goodness. It is therefore somewhat anthropomorphic to speak of an "act" of God's freedom. God can be nothing but God—yet he is not by the fact determined in his being. He cannot help his essential goodness—he remains unspeakably free. Freedom, we might venture, has something to do with being truly oneself—consciously, deliberately, *voluntarily* being all that one is called to be.

> I have already asserted previously that the freedom of a being, in the proper sense of the word, is its capacity to fulfill the law of its being and to fix and secure itself in it (as the principle which posits and gives form to it), i.e. to realize and establish itself in it.[3]

Or, if we consider freedom as a dimension of the personality, it is the dynamic process by which a responsible agent directs himself toward his final completion.

A second "species" of freedom is found in the classical theology of the angels. Again according to Aquinas, freedom in the angels is a quasi-infinite, instantaneous actualization of the total being of the angelic spirit-substance. Because of the power of the angelic intellect and the intensity of its will-act, confirmation in eternal goodness or evil (in other words, the irrevocable and voluntary self-actualization of the angel) is a necessary consequence of its *first choice* with respect to its final end.

The third and last species of freedom is that which is characteristic of man. Man is truly free. He certainly possesses something of that perfection which is found analogously in God and the angels. But his freedom is specifically human. Unlike an angel, man cannot totally commit himself in any one particular act. He cannot even realistically know what his purpose is in life all at once. It begins to dawn on him little by little, over a long period of maturation, through many errors, blind-alleys, and occasional successes. It is not enough to say that the revelation of the Gospel shows man what he is and what he must become, thus sparing him the painful and uncertain process of discovering it for himself. It is true that a man can be *told* about the Christian message. He can be *instructed* about the manner in which he ought to proceed in order to save his soul. But the exhortations must remain ineffectual until their full import is personally grasped in daily experience. And this is not a matter of days. It is a developmental process spanning years, perhaps decades.

The utterly gratuitous, almost blasphemous way in which we commonly use the term "mortal sin" does violence to the wisdom and mercy of God and to the nature of man. Schoonenberg is sensible on this point. In his book *Man and Sin* he says that man passes from venial to mortal sin and then to wickedness and the "sin unto death." But this is not done in a single act.

> Hence it is not enough *now* to perform a certain good work, a "basic good choice" in order to obtain heaven as a reward. One must also continue to correspond with the basic graces of perseverance. A parallel case exists for evil: it is not enough to commit a mortal sin in order to be punished with hell: man must also afterwards continue to reject the grace of conversion. . . . The basic moral acts and the mortal sins prepare us for the last good or evil choice in death and for its prefigurations during life. Thus man expresses himself always more deeply and determines himself always more completely through his free decision, either in the good by passing from "daily good action" to "basic moral acts," and from the latter to total self-donation and love, or in evil by passing from venial sin to mortal sin, and from the latter to integral wickedness, impenitence, and the "sin unto death."[4]

SERIOUS MORAL EVIL

What Catholic theology has termed "mortal sin" is, dogmatically, the subjective idolatrous elevation of a finite good to the level of one's "ultimate concern"—to borrow a phrase of Tillich's. When persevered in, this is spiritual death. It is even a kind of psychic death; for any attempt to discover the ultimate meaning of human existence in something essentially limited is to encounter despair. Perhaps the best current illustration of this are the films by Antonioni, Bergman, and Fellini.

It has often been said that, strictly speaking, the Greeks did not know sin, although they were conscious of moral imperatives, because sin must involve a personal relationship with God. Karl Rahner has pointed out the nature of theological guilt for sin.

> Guilt in the theological sense is not an offense against some universal custom, civic morality, public penal laws or conventions, the laws and conventions arising from normal upbringing, etc. Nor is it merely a wrong action with harmful, destructive, pathogenic, physically and socially disturbing effects. Sin and guilt in the theological sense are to be found only where man, addressed by God, acts in God's sight and together with him (as is his will), even though the overriding refusal to admit this fact and the suppression of this truth is one of the essential moments of guilt. Only when someone sins knowingly against God can there be guilt. It is quite a different matter to determine the extent to which there must be subjective and reflective "awareness" of saying "no" to God and his will and of thus (and only thus) establishing guilt.[5]

Theological guilt must also be very carefully distinguished from the feeling of guilt dealt with in psychology. Theological guilt is always a *conviction* of the mind—an often "cold-blooded" awareness of having transgressed the law of God in some way. The term "grave sin" is best used to refer to an act which objectively disrupts the moral order in a serious way; subjectively considered, it must be something sufficiently important or serious that it can be made—realistically—the basis of one's choice to love it in opposition to the will of God. This is the "matter" of sin.

The mutual causality that exists between the externalized act, material sin, and the subjective dispositions that inform it, making it human, can hardly be over-stressed. There has perhaps been undue emphasis in modern theology upon the subjective factors involved in sin as a reaction against the legalistic, act-oriented thinking of so much post-reformation moral theology. The subjective dispositions alone determine the degree of the sinner's guilt, but the externalization of those dispositions (the act of sin) profoundly determines the future course and intensity of the sinner's dispositions.

The scholastic distinction between material and formal sin has real merit. While many of a person's objectively bad actions may be guiltless before God, they are not harmless. Ignorance, lack of freedom, etc., rob the action of malice (formal sin). Nevertheless, some degree of damage has been done in the depths of the personality (if the act was strictly interior or private) and perhaps also in the area of human relations (if the act was overt). Such negative consequences of subjectively guiltless human actions still have something to do with morality—they are still "sinful" in some real sense. To say, for example, that the masturbation of an adolescent addicted to the practice is not formally (subjectively) sinful is not to say all that must be said about sin in his case. Unwittingly, guiltlessly perhaps, but surely, he is committing himself to a kind of psychosexual habit from which he can extricate himself only with more or less serious difficulty. Although the individual acts of masturbation may not be seriously important in themselves, the pattern can be very serious.

We especially want to avoid all theological voluntarism here. Sin is properly sin because it is opposed to the will of God. But this "will of God" is neither arbitrary nor vindictive. Following the thought of Aquinas, we see that the divine will is really identical with the true good of man. Sin is "contrary" to the "law of God," because it is first of all contrary to the good of man. Even the fact of special divine revelation does not alter this statement. The Church has repeatedly condemned the tempting proposition that certain acts can be theologically sinful while being philosophically (ethically) justifiable. In this context, it is worthwhile to repeat our basic premise: good morality and good psychology cannot be in conflict. There is no contradiction between the supernatural good of man and his ethical good. Rather, the view of man revealed in Sacred Scripture is a prolongation, a deepening and intensification of the picture of man described by the conscientious humanist.

As we mentioned above, a certain relationship to God is necessary before there can be the possibility of committing sin. But it would seem that a wholly *implicit*, non-reflexive notion of God is enough. For every man, the ultimate end of life is perfect happiness sought in love of another person. For the Jew, Muslim, or Christian, that perfect happiness is consciously and directly sought in the love of the God who has revealed himself in salvation history. For other mature human beings, who do not formally acknowledge a personal God, the case is different. Whatever it is that is the supreme Other-than-self demanding his ultimate conscientious loyalty is Deity. Deliberately to betray this loyalty is to sin seriously.

SIN AS ORIENTATION

We are primarily concerned here with subjective sin: what it is (theologically and psychologically), its degrees, and the conditions under which it may be "committed." To clarify matters a bit, we propose the following working definition: *Subjectively grave* (mortal) *sin is a fundamental orientation of mind, consciously and deliberately maintained in opposition to what one simultaneously perceives clearly to be the true purpose and aim of one's life.*

Subjectively serious sin is a fundamental orientation of mind. Theology which bases itself exclusively upon the Bible has little trouble with this statement. In Scripture, sin is invariably a *posture* before God. Its opposite is "righteousness" or "justice."[6] The *koine* Greek term "metanoia," used throughout the New Testament, indicates the process of turning from sin to God and signifies a profound change of mind and heart. In scholastic theology the very fact that mortal sin is defined as turning away from God as one's final end means that such sin implies a very basic, fundamental option. Sin of this nature, then, is an attitude of mind in radical opposition to the mind of God.

Such a fundamental human option, to be truly moral, must be accompanied by properly evaluative insight and reflection. This is not a simple matter to measure. Many of our decisions of lesser importance involve a high degree of insight and reflection. The more consequential the choice, though, the more difficult and involved the reflection becomes. One chooses a dinner menu or movie very deliberately, but with relative ease. The process of making a decision about taking a certain job or buying a home is more difficult and lengthy. There is more weighing of alternatives, more indecision. The really significant decisions in life, i.e., choosing a marriage partner, entering a profession—involve increasingly more tortuous decision processes. It hardly seems possible that the decision about heaven or hell, to serve or reject God, can be simply made.

A fundamental orientation of mind is hardly something that can take place in an instant or in any single "act." Human freedom characteristically asserts itself only through the pattern emerging out of many acts, each one of which is largely determined (nonfree) by its precedents. Louis Monden describes this well in *Sin, Liberty and Law*.

> Classical moral theology contains a treatise *"de impedimentis libertatis"* (on the obstacles to freedom) which applies not only within moral doctrine, but also within ecclesiastical legislation. It may even, to a great extent, have been transposed from jurisprudence to moral doctrine. A distinction is made between obstacles coming from within, mainly ignorance and the violence of instinctual impulses, and obstacles coming from without, mainly moral coercion, deceit and intimidation (vis et metus). In the light of the latest findings, however, these positions appear to be completely outmoded. They take for granted that man's freedom is a *perfectly autonomous power of decision*, hindered in the exercise of its sovereignty only accidentally, by factors which, although possibly often at work, remain by their nature exceptional. Quite different is the picture drawn by *contemporary anthropology*. Here freedom is seen as freedom in situation, and the dialectic of freedom and determinism is considered essential for every human action. Only this dialectic makes freedom into really human freedom, and modern science seems to find it more difficult to preserve the moment of freedom than to point out all that is determined in human activity.[7]

Some of the terms used in our definition of grave moral evil, or long range sin, need some elaboration from a psychological point of view. Before we present evidence to substantiate the definition, it should be clear just what our definition does and does not mean. When we refer to a "fundamental orientation" we mean the deepest and strongest commitment to a way of life, to a set of values and attitudes concerning moral behavior. This framework of habits, values, and attitudes is relatively stable and enduring. It is not acquired in a moment, nor changed in a month. Each moral situation and experience that occurs acts as a reinforcement for this orientation, making it more difficult to change. Moral orientation is analogous to occupational or professional identity in the sense that it is an important part of the individual's self-concept and can motivate behavior without conscious reflection. It is analogous to attitudes of bigotry, in that rational appeal to change stands little chance of success, because the foundation is composed of drives and emotions, rather than of reason. Orientation is the key concept in the analysis of moral behavior and will be discussed at length shortly.

When we refer to an attitude as "consciously and deliberately maintained" we are not speaking of a constant state of awareness. This orientation would enjoy approximately the same state of consciousness as one's occupational identity and goals; that is, certain situations and cues will, from time to time, demand that some temporary conscious attention be directed to the goal, the means, and the total orientation. Otherwise, it functions in a preconscious manner, dormant but powerful. This occasional awareness is sufficient for conscious maintenance of the orientation. In fact, there are very few long range aspects of life that are attended to very frequently or with great intensity of consciousness.

We will show later that a state of personal grave moral evil must be an ego-syntonic orientation; that is, it must be perceived by the person as an integral part of himself and accepted as such. It may be rationalized as the only way to get ahead, or the only way to deal with an essentially hostile world, or the only sensible response when life is so short. But however the defense may be phrased, there is no true conflict within the individual between his idea of himself and this moral orientation. There may be brief flickers of remorse or disapproval, but these are dismissed or suppressed. The person is not motivated to take steps to change his behavior and attitudes. More importantly, he is not greatly upset by the perceived discrepancy between himself and what he recognizes as the good. Conversely, we will show that that "state of grace," phenomenologically speaking, is also an orientation, that it is part of the very personality of the individual. It, too, functions through habits, values, and attitudes, giving direction to one's life, but not by means of constant conscious reflection.

MORAL HABITS

We must now consider the psychological and social errors embodied in traditional moral teachings. The traditional definition of serious sin had included the element of deliberation. This is defined as intellectual advertence to the gravity of the act, an evaluative apprehension of the moral danger, and the judgment whether to proceed or retreat. This type of definition presupposes a view of man as almost entirely rational. According to this viewpoint, alcohol, fatigue, or strong passion may occasionally intrude and becloud the intellect; but by and large man is credited with a great deal of voluntary control of his judgments, attitudes, and behavior. He would be aware of the moral implications of an act, free to decide in which way to act (or if he should act at all), and capable of a high degree of control over his impulses.

The facts are at odds with this view, particularly in terms of deliberation. For the deliberation spoken of in traditional definitions is *deliberation in the situation.* Once an individual is in the presence of a tempting object, or the moment that a wish-fulfilling fantasy is present in consciousness, he has passed the threshold of objective, consciously free deliberation. With every passing instant, he becomes more and more emotionally preoccupied, less and less capable of reflection, deliberation, and judgment. Responsibility is attenuated as feelings are aroused. If an individual is not constantly on guard, ready to suppress a fantasy instantly, change the subject of conversation, or leave a situation, it is easy to see that rational deliberation becomes rapidly overwhelmed by the arousal of drives and feelings. There is some psychological validity in the traditional advice on handling "bad thoughts" which urges an immediate displacement by prayer or some innocuous fantasy.

The facts support our assertion that deliberation concerning a moral act is at best short-lived and almost automatic. The economics of time and energy militate against a reflective, deliberative, long-range decision in every morally relevant situation. If the alternatives are to be weighed, the consequences assessed, and the judgment pondered, it is, in most cases, no longer a free decision. Time spent in a situation cumulates against a decision in favor of the good.

When we consider an individual who consistently makes decisions in favor of moral good rather than evil, it is obvious that we are speaking of someone who has *developed a moral habit*. This person does not, when confronted with a moral situation, speculate about the alternatives. It is psychologically impossible. In the lives of morally good persons, there are very few discrete, conscious, deliberate long range judgments in favor of the good. The individual operates in moral situations no differently than he does in other situations. He has made a prior decision, based partly on conscious deliberation about principle, and in greater part, on his total moral orientation. This orientation is not composed of a summation of prior judgments about specific moral acts. The moral orientation is not purely rational and conscious, but is itself composed of conscious, preconscious, and unconscious attitudes, values, fears, conflicts, and defenses. These elements interact and reinforce one another. The strength and momentum of the basic orientation is reinforced each day as minor temptations are resisted and good works performed.

The moral orientation is the most fundamental commitment a man can make. It pervades all areas of functioning. It transcends other goals by reason of its direction toward the final end; just as a person with the goal of a college education will subordinate other goals to this end, such as delaying marriage or tolerating economic hardship. It is the substance of man's morality, reflected in acts which are manifestations of it, but which remain only isolated, accidental indications, not in themselves sufficient to change it.

COMPONENTS OF MORAL ORIENTATION

The strength, endurance, and resistance to change of a person's moral orientation can be best understood by an analysis of the major factors which constitute it. Before the total orientation can change, there must be significant change in the habits, values, and attitudes that form it.

The major behavioral factor in a person's moral orientation is the cluster of habits relating to moral matters. These are predispositions to respond in a given way to situations. They have their roots in early childhood and are reinforced by situations, social pressure, and the person's values. Beginning with the preverbal training of the toddler in completely amoral matters such as not playing in the street, rudimentary table manners, and toilet training, habits of obedience and conformity are established. Although any parent will testify to the less than perfect obedience of children, he must admit that with increasing age, each situation demanding a response from the child is not totally unpredictable. The child's responses generalize from the specific content of warnings and prohibitions to authority and commands in general. That is, the child does not learn merely to clean up his room or not to run in the street, but learns a habit of obedience.

Each specific act which is in accord with parental wishes and values is reinforced through reward, strengthening the predisposition to respond in that manner to any situation perceived as similar. After the person has matured to the level at which the principles and values have become internalized, the reinforcement becomes internal also. The person will experience a feeling of righteousness and self-worth when he responds to a situation according to his principles. A common experience is noticing that a clerk has given too much change and, although the opportunity to cheat without fear of discovery is present, returning the money. The resulting feeling or glow is a powerful reinforcement. In time the habit of responding in accord with principle, although never totally uniform, becomes semi-automatic; the person does not weigh the antecedents, alternatives, and consequences prior to acting.

Important as habits are, they are only the observable, behavioral manifestations of the interior, relatively more enduring realities of value and attitude. In fact, moral habits are not completely trans-situational; that is, despite a strong moral habit, a person often responds differently to similar situations. Beginning with H. Hartshorne and M. A. May's *Studies in Deceit*[8] and continuing through the present, the research in moral behavior has revealed a disturbingly low correlation among moral choice situations and, consequently, low predictive value in assessments of the strength of moral habits. What this means realistically and practically is that knowledge of a person's response to one moral situation, such as returning excess change to a cashier, does not help too much in predicting whether that same person will cheat on his income tax or "borrow" tools from his shop. The problem in much of this research has been a focus on one or two personality variables, such as an easily measured moral habit or the level of moral thinking. The complex cluster of habits, values, attitudes, level of adjustment, and personality conflicts and defenses that make up a moral orientation must be taken into consideration. For example, an individual who would not keep an extra dollar from a chasier may well lie about his income tax deductions to the tune of five hundred dollars. A knowledge of the strength of his moral habit of honesty would not predict this. It becomes more understandable, however, if we are able to assess his attitudes toward institutions, governmental waste, the justice of taxation, and particularly his views on those who cheat cashiers as opposed to those who "fudge" on their taxes.

The tandem factors of value and attitude are the motive strength behind a moral habit. A person's hierarchy of values strongly influences the attitudes he holds toward various actions, situations, or classes of behavior. It is in this area that we have an apparent contradiction. Earlier we have insisted that a person acts as a whole, a unified organism-personality-self, not part-by-part. However, there can be compartmentalized, isolated, almost contradictory values and attitudes existing side by side. An example is the person who would not cheat on his income tax because he views it as a necessary, albeit painful, obligation which produces a good return in governmental services. This same person, however, may feel that insurance companies are directed by unprincipled bandits who are motivated solely by greed and therefore would adopt an isolated attitude of justified economic warfare in which the rules of honesty are suspended.

Extremely powerful, relatively unconscious attitudes are often the determining factor in what appears to be a moral decision. Racial bigotry may prompt unusually hostile behavior in one person, while a strong negative attitude toward authority may lead another to participate generously in civil rights activities. Because of training both at home and at school, certain moral values can become attached to specific acts, while the implications or consequences of the act are ignored. Many persons attach a negative moral evaluation to an act such as getting drunk at a party. They feel personally ashamed and even morally guilty enough to confess it. How much evil there is in an occasional lack of prudence or discretion is debatable and depends on the individual. But there is no question of the grave moral evil in driving home drunk after that party, placing lives in jeopardy. Yet this is a rarely admitted offense. Similarly, few persons view driving as morally relevant in any respect, despite the obvious responsibility. If an area of behavior, or specific acts, has not been labeled properly during the development of moral thinking, it is likely to remain isolated throughout the person's life. Conversely, unless specific values are labeled properly, they will remain abstract and have little conscious effect on behavior.

The attitudes and values that result from a person's social class, education, economic position, and occupation are a strong, generally unconscious constraint upon choice of behavior. In most lower and many working-class families, aggressive impulses are generally carried out through fighting. Most middle-class persons, on the other hand, have a difficult time remembering the last physical fight that they had. Masturbation is viewed much more tolerantly in middle- and upper-middle-class families than in lower-class families where it is often seen as a perversion. An individual's response to a moral choice situation is necessarily influenced, below the level of awareness, by social factors such as group pressure, shame, fear of ridicule, and strong identification with particular group values.

The most individual part of a person's moral orientation is the specific conflicts and psychological defenses that the person has developed throughout his life. If particular impulses or feelings are a source of anxiety to the person, he must develop defenses to ward off the anxiety. The more severe the conflict is over the expression of these impulses, the more rigid the defenses will become and the more distorted that person's perception of reality will be. Individuals with severe conflicts around sexual feelings can defend against anxiety in many ways. By repressing sexual feelings, the individual denies awareness of his impulses and must necessarily deny some sexual components in life situations. Much more common is the less severe type of conflict which leads to shame and embarrassment over normal, appropriate sexuality. Many defense mechanisms are used to avoid anxiety, and, most importantly, they become a fixed part of the person's moral orientation. Conflicts and defenses will be discussed in greater detail later in regard to specific problems.

CHANGE OF MORAL ORIENTATION

Granted that a person's moral orientation is composed of several factors, how resistant are these factors to change? Practically speaking, how easy or difficult is it for a person to shift his orientation from God to evil or vice versa? Is it true that a person can commit a morally evil act sufficient to condemn him on a Friday, return to the love of God on Saturday, then fall into serious moral evil during the following week? And can this be repeated month after month? Can Catholics commit mortal sins, confess them, and repeat this sequence several times a year? Our position is that this is impossible. The psychological evidence is incontrovertible: man is a creature of multidetermined habits, action and reaction patterns, values and attitudes, conflicts and defenses. Orientation toward a goal, commitment of oneself along any path that represents a vital, long range decision is not done in an instant, a day, a week, or probably even in a year, but is a gradual, cumulative, developmental process.

One area of strong evidence for the endurance of an orientation comes from the large body of research in psychotherapy. In this instance, it is important to realize that the person is *actively* trying to change certain habits and attitudes that are interfering with

personal happiness and satisfaction. In this discussion we are not
speaking of psychotic or severely neurotic individuals, for everyone
recognizes the tenacity of these extreme problems. We are not
appealing to evidence from psychopathology to support assertions
about the average person. Many, many persons are in psychotherapy today with the goal of working out a more satisfactory life
for themselves. These individuals have problems of one kind or
another with authority, close interpersonal relationships, dependency, sex, aggression, or achievement, or an existential crisis, but
are not afflicted with striking or interfering symptoms. It is this
group of relatively normal persons with problems, rather than
"problem persons," that reflect the difficulties in orientation change
of the average person.

It is clear from the studies of personality change in psychotherapy[9] that a significant change in personality, a restructuring
of basic attitudes and habits of reacting, is a long range accomplishment measurable in months and years, not days and weeks.
Some dramatic changes can take place in psychotherapy in a short
time, but these are generally in the area of symptom removal or
anxiety reduction. The reorientation of a person's values, attitudes,
and habitual responses in any important area of life is not accomplished in much less than a year, usually much longer. Even when a
person desires to change with every conscious fiber of his being, the
change is resisted and takes a protracted period of time, involving
spurts and plateaus, progress and relapses.

In all the various theories of personality, each of which attempts to explain the complexity of the human person, there is one
indisputable fact, and that is that each person exhibits continuity
and consistency over time. Although each theory employs different,
sometimes apparently contradictory hypotheses and constructs, all
agree on the fact that personality functions are relatively enduring
and that long range commitments involving the self are not made
or changed in one act.[10] Research in the area of social psychology
demonstrates the endurance of habits, attitudes, and values.[11] In
no instance does the research hint that a long range important
decision or orientation is made or changed in a short time. In the
area of occupational choice, the basic assumption is that needs,

values, attitudes, and interests are long-lived, not subject to capricious changes. Once a basic aptitude is demonstrated, the screening and counseling in this area focusses upon these variables.[12]

Perhaps the most compelling evidence for the consistency and continuity of orientation is each person's own history of major commitments. Very few persons are knocked off a horse by a lightning bolt these days. In most cases, a person remembers a long developmental process leading to a decision about the choice of a spouse or profession. Each person likewise has an idea about his moral orientation. Most individuals feel that they are oriented to God as their final end and that the sins they commit are accidents or remorseful incidents that have not shaken their orientation. Unfortunately, many people feel that once they have committed a serious act against God's law, they are by that one act liable to condemnation, and so they continue for a while on the theory that they may as well hang for a sheep as a lamb. This attitude, however, may be directly attributed to those who have been responsible for the moral education of the faithful and have focused their efforts on the act as the moral vehicle. For most persons, even when they have committed a serious sin, they feel that this is an exception, not the rule.

What then happens if a person who has been oriented to God for his lifetime succumbs to temptation? Given antecedent conditions of some sexual deprivation or an accumulation of resentments, he does not immediately reject a situation offering some immoral gratification of sexual or aggressive impulses. Resistance weakens as his preoccupation grows, and he chooses evil over good, resulting in serious sin. Has this one isolated instance reoriented this person's moral orientation 180 degrees away from God? It would seem from traditional definitions of mortal sin that this indeed occurred and that this person, by this one deliberate act, has condemned himself if he should die the next moment.

It seems obvious from the theological and psychological arguments above that there can be no act such that its commission or omission alone is mortally sinful, that by itself would condemn a person. Rather, grave moral evil lies in a pattern, a process, a habit of seriously evil acts, each of which reflects the person's basic moral orientation. A person who performs an act, regardless of its gravity, and is remorseful for it afterward because it is at odds with his orientation toward God, has not radically changed his orientation and has not committed a mortal or long-range sin.

Two crucial considerations, however, apply to the judgment of an act in its relation to an orientation. First, although the orientation cannot shift radically because of one act, it is nevertheless weakened by even materially sinful acts. Hence, a firm purpose of amendment must be translated into behavior. The person is responsible to see that a pattern does not build up. He must actively take steps to change those aspects of his life that weaken the orientation. This imposes a mature, adult moral responsibility upon the person. Strong, even emotional resolutions to do better are worthless unless they can be applied to specific patterns of behavior. In sexual matters, as we shall discuss in the following chapters, a firm purpose of amendment must take forms such as shifting from single to group dates, avoiding drive-in movies, or other tactical changes in behavior. To hope that a mental resolution, even one buttressed by prayer, will keep one from repeating previously enjoyed forbidden activities is psychologically and morally absurd.

Second, and more importantly, acts which are themselves not grave or serious, but nevertheless are against the law of God, can little by little over a long period of time shift an orientation completely away from God into grave moral evil. Traditional moral theology has held that any number of venial sins do not add up to a mortal sin. This holds only when the act is the focus of morality. This is not true when the person and his total moral orientation are considered. A minor fault of insensitivity to the rightful needs of others can grow into inconsiderateness. This habit easily deepens into self-centered lack of concern for others and ultimately hardens into a rejection of God's law. A person can, without ever committing an overtly grave or materially mortal sin, certainly turn completely away from God into a state of grave moral evil or long range sin.

This thesis, that a person cannot condemn himself by one act regardless of its gravity yet can slip into that state by a multitude of lesser acts, will be applied to specific problems in the following chapters. Because sexuality is such a moral labyrinth for most persons, married or single, we will focus on various aspects of this problem.

NOTES TO CHAPTER TWO

1. Letter of Claudius Aquaviva, April 24, 1612, as quoted in J. Noonan, *Contraception* (New York: New American Library, 1965), 428.

2. P. Schoonenberg, *Man and Sin* (Notre Dame, Ind.: Notre Dame Press, 1965).

3. F. von Baader, *Samtliche Werke*, ed. F. Hoffman, J. Hamberger, and others (Aalen: Scientia Publishers, 1963), 302.

4. Schoonenberg, *op. cit.*, 39.

5. K. Rahner, "Forgotten Truths Concerning the Sacrament of Penance," in *Theological Investigations* (Baltimore: Toplinger, 1963), II, 266-267.

6. A. Gelin and A. Descamps, *Sin in the Bible*, trans. by C. Schaldenbrand (Paris: Desclee Co., 1960), II, 40.

7. L. Monden, *Sin, Liberty and Law* (New York: Sheed and Ward, 1965), 20.

8. H. Hartshorne and M. A. May, *Studies in Deceit* (New York: Macmillan, 1928).

9. G. E. Stollak, B. G. Guerney, and M. Rothberg, *Psychotherapy Research: Selected Readings* (Chicago: Rand-McNally, 1966); J. D. Frank, *Persuasion and Healing: A Comparative Study of Psychotherapy* (Baltimore: Johns Hopkins Press, 1961); P. H. Hoch and J. Zubin (eds.), *The Evaluation of Psychiatric Treatment* (New York: Grune & Stratton, 1964).

10. G. W. Allport, *Personality: A Psychological Interpretation* (New York: Holt, 1937); J. Dollard and N. E. Miller, *Personality and Psychotherapy: An Analysis in Terms of Learning, Thinking and Culture* (New York: McGraw-Hill, 1950); S. Freud, *The Standard Edition of the Complete Psychological Works*, ed. J. Strachey, (London: Hogarth Press, 1953); K. Goldstein, *The Organism* (New York: American Book Co., 1939); H. A. Murray and collaborators, *Explorations in Personality* (New York: Oxford, 1938); C. R. Rogers, *Client-centered Therapy; Its Current Practice, Implications, and Theory* (Boston: Houghton-Mifflin, 1951).

11. I. A. Berg and B. M. Bass (eds.), *Conformity and Deviation* (New York: Harper, 1961); G. W. Allport, *The Nature of Prejudice*

(Reading, Mass.: Addison-Wesley, 1954); A. R. Cohen, *Attitude Change and Social Influence* (New York: Basic Books, 1964); M. J. Rosenberg, C. I. Hovland, and others, *Attitude Organization and Change* (New Haven, Conn.: Yale University Press, 1960).

12. L. J. Cronbach, *Essentials of Psychological Testing* (2nd ed.; New York: Harper, 1960); E. K. Strong, *Vocational Interests of Men and Women* (Stanford: Stanford University Press, 1943).

CHAPTER THREE

SEXUALITY AND MORAL LIVING

THE PRINCIPLES DEVELOPED in the preceding two chapters might be applied very fruitfully to areas of moral concern such as the control of hostility and aggression. Sexuality, however, is such an essential dimension of human functioning and so crucial to the development and maintenance of a proper life-orientation that it warrants a key position in any discussion of personal moral behavior. The problem of integrating sexuality into one's total orientation is, at best, fraught with serious difficulties. Nevertheless, it is a problem that everyone has to face and solve if he expects to achieve some measure of happiness in life. Sexuality is so central to a person's functioning in every area of life that a moral problem involving sexuality must inevitably permeate many other aspects of moral behavior. It is important to realize that we are not trying to defend a "pansexualist" theory of motivation, but rather to place sexuality in what we consider to be a proper perspective for moral consideration and to evaluate its influence upon other aspects of a person's life. Marc Oraison asserts:

> What the clinical psychologist indicates by the words "sexuality" or "sexual drive" goes far beyond the ordinary meaning of these words. We are concerned with a basic and very general emotional energy— psychological in the wide sense—of which the genital aspect is only the culminating and, so to speak, specialized manifestation. . . . If we understand by "pansexualism" a theory that tends to reduce

every human expression, even the highest expressions of the mind, to an unconscious response of the genital sexual order, then it is understandable that such a view should be found excessive and revolting. But this is not what Freudian psychology means by sexuality. We must also note that Freud himself, in spite of disputable philosophical a priori's and inadmissible speculative extrapolations, was never pansexualist in this narrow sense.[1]

Sexual drives form a major part of man's impulse life and they exert varying degrees of influence upon most of his thoughts and actions. We are considering not only the direct, conscious effect of sexuality upon the diverse activities in which man engages. Sexuality vitally influences and determines fantasies and actions in many unconscious, indirect ways. Most sublimations, expressions, and gratifications of the sex drive are decidedly not overt or conscious; nor do they necessarily reflect genitally heterosexual impulses aimed at intercourse (a commonly understood meaning of "sex"). Friendship, companionship, aesthetic forms of emotional expression, attitudes toward achieving objectives or retreating from them, manners of speech and dress are only a few of the many possible manifestations of sexual impulses.

A person's sex determines a great many of the rules which will govern his upbringing in different cultures and subcultures. A young boy in our culture, for instance, is raised according to the principle that men are supposed to control the expression of their emotions in a way that is not expected of women. Boys do not cry in public. The training for adult life as a man or woman produces a very early sex-role identification in the child. He or she is taught to assume different attitudes toward aggression, achievement, passivity, work, emotional expression, dress, and so forth. Sexual differences in the functioning of the endocrine system figure very importantly in determining those characteristics by which we commonly distinguish the sexes. Modern advances in steroid chemistry have made it possible to effect vast changes in personality by the administration of sex hormones. Most familiar, perhaps, are the wonderful results obtained through the use of estrogens in alleviating severe menopausal personality disturbances in women.

It is certainly not our contention that all or even most of man's activities are directly determined by sexual urges. The central position of sexuality in the full picture of human moral development is shown, rather, in this way: *central personality functions have a profound influence upon every human attitude, fantasy and action; these functions, in turn, are greatly determined by sexual impulses in their early formation and are constantly modified by general sexuality in their day-to-day interactions.*

PERSONALITY DEVELOPMENT

One example already mentioned is the individual's sex-role identification. Masculinity and femininity mean infinitely more than the differences in primary sex characteristics. Being "man" or "woman" refers to basic polarities in the very nature of human beings; they are the basic causes and expressions of the difference and complementarity which is the very essence of "being human."

> We have long heard talk of "gradations" and of the "relativity" of sex, ideas difficult to fit into our ways of speech. They upset a number of static images based on unreasoned sentiments, on custom, and on the male fear of losing the absolute character of the organ that makes him "male." But, biologically speaking, we cannot speak of maleness or femaleness as characteristics that are fixed and defined in isolated individuals; we are dealing rather with the reciprocity of functions.[2]

Further highlighting the importance of sexuality for all human growth and endeavor, Oraison says:

> Yet it is beyond question that the whole personality, even in its most developed, its most specifically human—that is to say, spiritual—manifestations, is impregnated and conditioned by the evaluation and modalities of its "desire to love and be loved"—each according to his proper sex. All behavior, even the highest intellectual behavior, is unavoidably colored by the existential attitude of relation that establishes the subject—as the man he is or as the woman she is—in dialogue with the world; is colored, therefore, in the Freudian sense, by his sexuality.[3]

Another aspect of personality that exercises a high degree of control over man's behavior is the way in which he most consistently regards himself—the self-image or self-concept. It is impossible to separate this vitally important dynamism from sexuality. The self-concept is a pattern of memories, perceptions, attitudes, and so forth that stabilizes the personality by giving it a certain historical continuity and the consequent ability to act in a more or less consistent fashion. That is, a person recognizes that he is the same person he was ten years ago (allowing, of course, for maturation and change). He has attitudes toward himself (some of which may not be objectively substantiated) which largely determine his attitudes toward other people and things, his goals, values, and fantasy life. W. E. Henry states:

> There are two special features of the personality tendency toward consistency. . . . These features are: first, *a resistance to repeated change*, and second, *a tendency to reproduce itself.* This first tendency is a direct reflection of the development of consistency within the personality and the gradual reduction over time of the ability of the personality to change. As consistency develops, flexibility decreases. With this reduced flexibility, an additional feature appears, the tendency to reaffirm the present consistency.[4]

A person's self-concept and sex-role identification begin in infancy. The tiny infant experiences the world in a way that is almost purely physical. He is able to experience love only by such bodily contacts as nursing, being hugged, kissed, and so on. As far as the infant is concerned, love is coextensive with physical affection. It is only much later that he learns to use words to convey his feelings. Very early in life the child's preoccupation with his body and its physiological functions encounters parental control in the form of restrictions—denials of his hitherto unrestrained self-gratification. Although mature sexuality is obviously not present, there are strong feelings and fantasies that can only be categorized as sexual. The attitudes which the child consequently adopts toward his body and toward the various feelings he experiences are a result of, and are reinforced by, parental reactions.

More specifically, the child's self-concept includes, in a very significant way, his attitude toward sexual impulses and their control. If a child's early curiosity about his body, his self-exploration and manipulations as well as the normal exploratory curiosity (not unmixed with real eroticism!) about the bodies of other children are met with shock, anger, or disgust on the part of the parents, his future attitudes toward sexuality will necessarily be negative. Later experiences or even fantasies which contain sexual elements will produce varying degrees of uneasiness, shame, and feelings of guilt. The child's self-concept will be distorted in the area of sexual impulses, and his reaction to sexual fantasies and feelings generally will be repressive and guilt-laden as a consequence of that distortion.

The adolescent or adult reacts to particular situations as a *total* personality. All of his attitudes, values, habits of thinking and acting, his self-concept and ideals interact with the particular given situation to produce the response. Even in relatively neutral or innocuous situations man's sexuality influences his behavior. Far below the level of genital arousal and in circumstances devoid of all perceptible sexual connotation, sexuality is nevertheless sublimated and gratified. Just as the mildest forms of self-assertion or competition are linked to aggressive impulses, so in a similar way, the simple pleasurable social interactions of everyday living are linked to sex drives. To amplify: just as in the ordinary give-and-take of daily life a person does not experience the aggressive impulse in its most recognizable forms such as rage or anger, so in the ordinary social pleasures of daily life he does not experience any conscious, overtly sexual feelings.[5]

Of course, any purely psychological approach to human sexuality must remain incomplete. Psychology studies the individual and formulates theoretical generalizations about individual behavior, motivation, and so forth. But the individual never exists in isolation; the matrix within which he is born, changes, and matures is always social. The moral development of the individual can never be abstracted from the context of general goals and values embodied in the larger society which nurtures him. Before proceeding to a discussion of sexuality and moral responsibility, then, we ought first to consider the relationship between individual ethical behavior and the ethics of society.

CULTURE AND THE INDIVIDUAL

Sociologically, we may define morality as a system of norms, mores, and values controlling behavior within a given culture in a way best suited to furthering the implicitly acknowledged aims of that culture. In the formation of the individual's moral orientation and behavior there is a dynamic interplay between the "morals" of the individual and the "morals" of society. In the process of socialization, the individual person *internalizes* to a very large extent the value-judgments of his culture. He is pressured to conform, more or less adequately, to the "code morality" of the larger society. Primary emphasis on objective conformity to social norms is what can be conveniently called "code morality"—the corporate society, not the individual, is the primary subject of rights and obligations. Code morality is found principally in primitive communitarian societies. It is also a dominant aspect of Marxist communism and (more commonly in the past than today) of religious orders in the Catholic Church.

If we examine for a moment the social psychology of the vows of religion (prescinding from whatever deeper theological import they may have), we are struck by the fact that each of the vows has as its objective the control of the potentially destructive spontaneous and instinctual life of the individual member,[6] ordering those lower impulses to the achievement of the higher good of the community. The vow of poverty, for instance, prevents the individual from accumulating and disposing of material goods in an individualistic, arbitrary fashion; wealth and its disposition rests in the community. Similarly, the vow of religious obedience tames and channels the self-assertive, aggressive drives of the individual, subordinating personal ambition to the achievement of communal goals. Finally, the vow of chastity harnesses the sexual dynamisms in the interest of communal harmony and charity. An underlying assumption in all this, of course, is that God's grace works most effectively where man's "concupiscence" is well-ordered and controlled.

Explicit vows of poverty, chastity, and obedience are defensible only from an ascetical and religious point of view. What is important to realize, though, is that the *functional equivalents* of these vows are absolutely indispensable controls upon the primitive instincts of the human animal (greed, lust, and aggression) which would, without such controls, threaten the existence of all society. Ideally speaking, the vows of religious life explicitly sublimate to an "heroic" degree what is implicitly demanded of every individual to a lesser extent in every culture. The cost of such societal control is not inconsiderable, however, for it involves the setting up of a kind of dialectic opposition between the individual's need for autonomous self-expression and the demands of life in society.

> When we survey the history of morality we can see that this interplay of morality and moral codes moves, through various fluctuations, in the direction of a constantly clearer and firmer assertion of a personalist morality over against a group morality. Contemporary man demands a personalist morality more universally and more intensely than ever. We see here, therefore, a dialectic process, a struggle between two tendencies, the result of which seems to show a more and more pronounced triumph of personalist morality, or in dialectical terms, a synthesis in which code morality is ousted by true morality.[7]

We would prefer to think that the results of this dialectical tension between the demands of the social code and the exigencies of personal liberty will not be the eventual "ousting" of code morality in favor of individual spontaneity, but that *the dialectic itself constitutes the basis of real morality whether communal or social*. Human freedom, the core of authentic morality ("personalist morality"), "is the capacity for something total. If it is to be able to bring about salvation or damnation, and thus to determine the whole man, it brings the whole man into play, in his past and in his future, in all the complexity of his self-world-God relationships."[8] True freedom is authentic self-realization, both a state of *being* human and a process of *becoming* ever more fully human. It is essentially bound up with the dialectical relationships between the individual and society. To deny, minimize or exaggerate either pole of this dialectic is to distort or destroy that human freedom without which there is no morality. The heresy of exaggerated emphasis on the social element apotheosizes the law and leads to slavery. The opposite heresy of extreme personalism culminates in a paranoid license.[9] We will return to this later.

EMOTIONAL STATES

In the dialogue of relations which mold his freedom, man always acts as a totality. There can never be a functional dichotomy between his affective, emotional life and his intellectual-volitional spiritual life. The psychology of psychosexual development clearly confirms our thesis that the attainment of mature moral awareness and responsible action begins with and is subsequently largely determined by the proper growth and functioning of the emotional life of the individual.

Recognition of the vital importance of the emotions in the moral life of man is, of course, not a particularly modern discovery. In his commentary on Aristotle's treatise *De Anima* and in the *Summa Theologiae*[10] St. Thomas Aquinas develops at great length an analysis of the two basic appetites (drives) in the sensitive (emotional) life of man. He derives all the human passions[11] from these two fundamental drives. The primary drive, or concupiscible appetite, is the pleasure-pain principle; it aims simply and directly at attaining the pleasurable good and avoiding the painful. The other fundamental drive, the irascible appetite, is distinct from the concupiscible appetite, but related to it; it comes into play to overcome obstacles which the pleasure-pain principle encounters in attaining its goals.[12] We do not know how attentively Freud read Aristotle or Aquinas, but his theory of instincts[13] bears a striking resemblance to the appetite theory of the philosophers. Freud's sexual drive (libido) is practically interchangeable with the concupiscible appetite of the scholastics, and his aggressive drive beautifully corresponds to what the medievals called the irascible appetite.

It would be indefensible to push this parallel too far for a number of reasons. The discovery of the dynamic unconscious is

Freud's—its analysis, unknown to the scholastics, made possible the richer understanding of man's psychic life so fruitfully being explored by modern depth psychologies. Medieval philosopher-theologians emphasized the freedom of man's will and his rational power of control over his emotions much more than modern psychology warrants.[14] But once we modify the exaggerated rationalism of medieval philosophical psychology and admit the crucial role of emotions in the moral life of man we can argue that our Freudian-like restatement of the centrality of the sexual (concupiscible) drive in the human personality is in no way a radical departure from broadly traditional thinking.

According to our modern understanding of man, the apparently discrete basic needs of self-preservation and self-propagation are found to be essentially *one*. Man preserves his physiological life by eating and drinking, but his physiological life is continuous with his emotional life (to which endocrinology so dramatically testifies), and his emotional life is continuous with his highest moral and spiritual activities. But in order to preserve his own life (in the fullest sense) man must love another; he really accomplishes self-preservation and self-fulfillment only *through* self-propagation. Here we understand self-propagation not as genital sexuality alone, but as the broadest extension of the sexual which is capable of being achieved either by direct expression or by various forms of sublimation. In his remarkable introduction to Abel Jeanniere's recent *Anthropology of Sex*, Sullivan aptly expresses the fundamental significance of the sexual for fully human existence:

> To say that romantic love between man and woman, understood as the ground of sexual union and abandon, nevertheless goes deeper and extends beyond the erotic, is not necessarily to make a distinction between Eros and Agape. Sexual desire and human desire are, in my opinion, one and the same with different moments only. In fact, the traditional understanding of Agape in God as pure and disinterested bestowal probably stemmed as much from the theologians' fear of a "sexy" God as from the notion of God as pure Act. Thus, Jeanniere rightly talks about love as a propensity in man's nature. Man simply cannot *not* love, and he must love "fully." Man must love because it is only there that, as Hegel observed, the mind

"feels its own unity." And as Jeanniere reminds us, pointing us back to that unreal state called "being in love," "every person learning to love knows that he is himself only with the other," and "for the lover there is no refuge in himself; he is truly what he is only before the other."[15]

MORALITY AND CULTURE

Human development is, in its beginnings, profoundly selfish. The embryonic personality is almost purely receptive and ingestive. All subsequent growth of the power to love involves the expansion of what is initially a self-oriented complex of needs to include the other-than-self. Eventually the relationships with the "other" culminate in the realization that "to be for another" is the only way a man can truly "be himself." Personal development, then, is inconceivable without socialization (the process of integrating the "other"), and the fundamental dynamism of this process is sexual. At birth the infant is a mass of amorphous energy (Freud's "id") which very soon becomes differentiated into the sexual and aggressive drives. Later growth and development of the self involves the constant shaping of these basic impulses toward an ever-increasing complexity and refinement. The progressive direction of future ego-development is greatly determined by preceding levels of development and is limited to a large extent by the cultural-moral level of the society into which the individual is born and within which he is formed.[16] But—and here we come to an important principle in our argument—*a high degree of cultural development is directly correlated with a correspondingly highly controlled expression of the basic human drives.*[17] Personal control and direction of these drives is a necessary requisite for social harmony and adequate role functioning. Primary among these drives is the sexual.

Ethnological research among peoples all over the world reveals several "cultural universals." These are traits, institutions or patterns of conduct which are found in one form or another in every human society without exception. Among these very few universals are marriage and the incest prohibition. Every theory which has tried to explain why incest (cross-culturally defined in various ways) is always and everywhere forbidden has proved to be somehow inadequate. Many of these theories have been based on social, economic or eugenic considerations. This perhaps accounts for their failure to explain fully the universality of such a prohibition. Something as ubiquitous as this must be explainable, not by factors which vary from culture to culture, but by a constant[18] in human nature itself.

We are aware of the fact that the possible existence of such a "constant" is disputed by social anthropologists. But by interpolating data from other disciplines such as philosophy and psychology, we believe that its existence must be postulated. If there is anything in the nature of man that is not produced by or dependent upon a particular culture, it is there that we might hope to find a solution to the problem.[19] Malinowski's explanation of the reasons for the incest taboo seem closest to what we have in mind. He says:

> The sexual impulse is in general a very upsetting and socially disruptive force, (it) cannot enter into a previously existing sentiment without producing a revolutionary change in it. Sexual interest is therefore incompatible with any family relationship, whether parental or between brothers and sisters . . . If erotic passion were allowed to invade the precincts of the home it would not merely establish jealousies and competitive elements and disorganize the family but it would also subvert the most fundamental bonds of kinship on which the further development of all social relationships is based . . . A society which allowed incest could not develop a stable family; it would therefore be deprived of the strongest foundations for kinship, and this in a primitive community would mean absence of social order.[20]

Following Malinowski's insight, then, the incest prohibition emerges as a social regulation of the raw sex drive making the family, the fundamental unit of human society, possible. Along with other regulations of sexuality, the incest taboo domesticates the animal urge for direct and indiscriminate sexual expression, controlling and channelling this energy to serve the higher goals of the family unit and the larger society. The more primitive the society is, the fewer are the controls needed, since only a fraction of the total available sexual energy is necessary to maintain other, non-specifically sexual structures. But as a given culture increases in the complexity of its role-functions, greater psychic-energy demands are made upon the members of the society. This energy is made available through the increased control and harnessing of libidinous and aggressive impulses. In a society as complex as twentieth-century America, the problem of utilizing sexual energies in a constructive way meets with serious difficulties.

One of the great crises in the contemporary American sociological scene is the so-called "identity crisis." Progressively greater demands are being made upon the individual to function in a greater number of roles, with a corresponding decrease of emotional satisfaction in any of them. The more he emotionally invests himself in this multiplicity of roles, the less able he is to find his "self" in any one of them. A South African Bushman has no such difficulties. His cultural sociology is such that he has only four basic and very uncomplicated roles. He is mate to his wife (husband role), shows special affection for his offspring and teaches them some basic skills (father role), provides his band with game, occasionally acts as defender to the little group and participates in general decision-making and settling of disputes (political-economic role). In the first two roles the expression of sexual dynamisms is obvious; in the third function the aggressive impulses are clearly operative.

All the role functions of the Bushmen are a relatively direct and therefore adequate and satisfying expression of the basic human drives. But in our own society roles tend to become less and less expressive of basic human needs. The process of rationalization—the separation of impulse-gratification from role-function—is at the bottom of both the identity-crisis syndrome and the contemporary sexual revolution. Personal feelings of discontent, anxiety, and frustration without any clearly assignable cause (the existentialists' "angst") are at least partially symptomatic of this cleavage between the erotic-aggressive impulses of man which can never be totally repressed and the opportunities which our society affords for their adequate, emotionally satisfying expression.

Authorities generally agree that sexual deviations are on the increase today. Such an increase in asocial sexual behavior is to be expected, since sexual deviations from generally accepted mores tend to increase in any given culture in direct proportion to the over-all complexity of the culture.[21] This is apparently due to the fact that in a complex society the sexual drive is diversified to furnish the dynamisms for many more societal functions than would be necessary for a simpler culture. Since the orgastic aspects of sexuality can erupt wherever an area of social interaction attempts to channel sexual (libidinal) energy, sexual deviations are relatively rare in very primitive cultures, while they are extremely prevalent (occasionally becoming legally sanctioned) in highly developed civilizations.

Individual control and direction of sexuality becomes increasingly urgent as society grows in complexity. Our contemporary Western civilization has intensified its technological complexity at an unprecedented, exponential rate during the last thirty years. Technology produces problems and poses questions for man, but it cannot solve them. Tragically, although predictably, our general culture has not been able to keep up—and it is the total cultural milieu which figures so importantly in the moral development of the individual. The internationalization of cultural values and norms which tends to establish the essential moral orientation of the individual can hardly occur if the disproportion between the individual's existentially perceived values and the culturally-embodied values of the society becomes too great.

A code morality which no longer represents the deepest (and therefore perennially valid) needs of the individual is "disfunctional." It is no longer really representative of the values, ideals, and goals of the individual person as he honestly experiences himself in relation to his environment and to his God (or equivalent ultimate value in life). Individual psychic controls have not only been unable to keep pace with the near-monstrous demands of modern technology and urbanization, but the very attempt to exercise any kind of control at all is in danger of being abandoned.

The old taboos which channeled free sexual energy into socially constructive endeavor are becoming increasingly useless today, for they were invented to serve a way of life that no longer exists. This poses an enormous problem. How can a young man or woman today hope to find a key to some kind of personal happiness and fulfillment by following a code of sexual conduct befitting a world-view that is no longer viable? It is quite understandable that leaders who naively insist on obedience to traditional norms without a back-up by reasonable motivations will be judged by our young people as stupid, hypocritical, or both. We cannot hope to replace the old taboos with new ones, for the myth-constructing forces of man's mind (upon which depend the origin of taboos with their peculiar compulsion toward certain patterns of behavior) have been prac-tically annihilated by the exorcisms of the modern sciences. What is left? Anarchy, possibly. Or the alternative possibility of rediscover-ing, with the help of the social sciences themselves, the universally valid kernels of practical wisdom that lie encapsulated in the out-moded shells of the old taboos.

Many otherwise responsible leaders, probably motivated as much by despair as by a desire to "relate" to young people, increasingly advocate a sexual permissiveness based on one or an-other formulation of what is popularly known as the "New Moral-ity." According to Joseph Fletcher, one of its most articulate champions in the United States, Christians and non-Christians alike should at least be able to agree on two basic principles of ethics. The first principle dictates that we should love people, not things; immorality is possible only when we invert this order and love things instead of people. Secondly, we should love people, not abstract rules or principles. What is really significant from an ethi-cal point of view is not any sort of hard-and-fast moral law, but rather what we can do for the good of others in any situation.[22] In enunciating these basic postulates of situation ethics, Fletcher is driving us down to the bedrock of personalist morality. He reminds us that genuine moral activity is the highest human activity. Fur-thermore, moral behavior springs from a full awareness of the need of the "other" with a free desire to meet that need by a loving, effective response. The full force of these principles has been buried for a long time in Catholic theology, and it is heartening to believe that its disinterment may help to restore both credibility and functionality to our sclerotic moral theology. But a purely situational morality cannot be the whole answer.

Applied to sex questions, Fletcher's approach seems to permit an isolation of sex and sexuality from the formation of the whole moral character of the individual in society. When he says, "character shapes sex conduct, sex does not shape character,"[23] he is ignoring an important principle of psychology: there is a reciprocal causality between "what one is" (character) and what one does. Certain actions, especially if frequently repeated, can strongly reinforce, even modify, attitudes and goals. Each time a person performs an action which he regards as subjectively significant, he endows the object of the action with a certain *value*. He necessarily perceives it as more or less important, else why would he do it? How important it is to him depends not only on the degree of importance of his motivation, but also upon *the degree of emotional energy expended upon and invested in the action.* Having performed the act, a complementary process of *internalization* occurs. He *identifies* with the act-value, and it becomes part of his "character." Considering the central importance of sex in the development of personality and character, the unique kind of total-person involvement that is inseparable from the act of intercourse, it is inconceivable that "character shapes sex conduct" but "sex does not shape character."[24]

Perhaps a certain qualification is in order here. We certainly wish to avoid a "mystical" approach to sex. That sort of thing has been a popular approach from time immemorial—most recently by some Catholic theologians who were trying to defend the Church's prohibition of artificial contraception.[25] As we tried to show in the previous chapter, a man never expresses himself fully in any single act. Neither does he definitively determine his sexual orientation by any particular act. *It is the pattern that is most important.* But while conduct-patterns are ultimately the only objective basis by which to evaluate the moral stance of the individual in his relationship to society, such conduct-patterns are personal *habits*. Whether we like it or not, habits or conduct-patterns are the externally observable correlatives of internal *orientations*, and these orientations can only be produced and sustained by individual acts.

We believe, therefore, that it is neither trite nor atavistic to attempt a serious reexamination of the moral norms which have traditionally guided sexual acts.

One final (and very practical) observation needs to be made. A progressively greater emancipation of marriage from economic necessities is a major factor in divorce today. Formerly marriages were chiefly socio-economic arrangements; romantic love was almost a side issue. But the modern equality of the sexes, a rapidly diminishing emphasis upon the home as the center of family activity, the economic independence of wives, fewer children and the lessening of the ties binding mother to child (suckling by bottle instead of breast, the institution of the "babysitter"), technological advances which progressively eliminate much of what was formerly essential to "keeping house"—all these factors contribute to a heightened focus upon the erotic-affectionate element in marriage.[26] But sexual eroticism is a very unstable, unpredictable thing. Unless we are prepared to part with the idea that a stable liaison between man and woman is necessary to the stability of society as a whole, we are forced to realize that a disciplined control of sexuality is a critical obligation for everyone. This is especially true of adolescents who are, by definition, in the process of forming the kind of sexual direction and control that will assure a relatively stable psycho-moral orientation later in their lives.

NOTES TO CHAPTER THREE

1. M. Oraison, *Illusion and Anxiety* (New York: The Macmillan Company, 1963), 104.
2. A. Jeanniere, *Anthropology of Sex* (New York: Harper and Row, 1967), 61-62.
3. Oraison, *op. cit.*, 105.
4. W. E. Henry, *The Analysis of Fantasy* (New York: Wiley, 1956), 7.
5. For a full treatment of the role of sexuality in the formation of attitudes, habits, values, goals, and self-concept—that is, the whole per-

sonality—see C. S. Hall and G. Lindsey, *Theories of Personality* (New York: Wiley, 1957), or any standard textbook of introductory psychology or developmental psychology.

6. "Three things especially may hinder (the religious') affection from being completely directed toward God: the concupiscence of the eyes, or the desire of exterior things, the concupiscence of the flesh, and the pride of life, the love of independence. These he renounces by the three vows. . . . He has nothing more that he can offer . . ." R. Garrigou-LaGrange, *Three Ages of the Interior Life*, (St. Louis: Herder, 1947), I, 216.

7. J. Walgrave, "Is Morality Dynamic or Static?" in *Moral Problems and Christian Personalism* (New York: Paulist Press, 1965), 32.

8. K. Rahner, "On the Theology of Freedom," in *Freedom and Man*, ed. J. C. Murray (New York: P. J. Kenedy, 1965), 210.

9. The history of heresies furnishes innumerable examples of the human tendency to prefer the comfortable simplicity of "either-or" thinking to the insecurities and ambivalences inherent in a "both-and" approach. Freedom is a living thing, and life is disequilibrium. To eliminate the dialectic by absolutizing either the individual or the community is to destroy that delicately balanced tension which is freedom's soul. Knox's *Enthusiasm* (Oxford University Press, 1950) is a near classic on this subject.

10. *Prima Secundae* Qq. 22-46.

11. "Passions" in Thomist philosophy are the various movements of the two-fold sense appetite, eleven in number. They range in intensity from barely perceptible feelings of aesthetic pleasure to the vehemence of uncontrollable rage.

12. For Aquinas as well as for Freud the concupiscible appetite (sexual drive) is logically and really prior; pleasure must first be experienced before obstacles to its attainment can be overcome.

13. At least one psychiatrist has found Thomistic psychology sufficiently in accord with Freudian dynamics to furnish a workable theoretical framework for psychotherapy. See A. A. A. Terruwe, *The Neurosis in Rational Psychology* (New York: P. J. Kenedy, 1960).

14. We must beware of hastily dismissing all scholastic psychology as overly rationalistic. Too often the Aristotelian-Thomistic tradition is caricatured by a facile identification with the worst elements of decadent scholasticism. The exaggerated dualism which separates soul from body, mind from senses, self from world, could not be more foreign to the thought of Aristotle or Aquinas. Unfortunately, the influence which dominated eighteen hundred years of Western intellectual history was not Aristotle, but the Platonic-Augustinian tradition which, after the thirteenth century, hybridized Aristotle to produce the sterile, nominalist syncretisms so aptly satirized by Erasmus. The obsession with distinctions, the talent for

analysis without synthesis so characteristic of the "either-or" mentality seduced philosophy away from a full openness to the complexity of truth to the false security of Cartesian "clear and precise ideas." Descartes' reduction of philosophy to the analytical exactitude of mathematics injected a slow-acting poison into metaphysics that eventually proved fatal. Mathematics has a validity and certitude apart from objective reality; its propositions are demonstrable by the mind alone. Aristotle taught that all knowledge came through the senses, and the first principle of knowledge and certitude followed immediately from the intellect's intuitive realization—via sense data—that "something *is*." But that would not do for Descartes; he could not trust the senses. One thing could not be doubted, however: "I *think*, therefore I am." This first principle of Cartesian philosophy breaks the link between intellect and *being*. It is only a matter of time until philosophy degenerates into a bewildering array of "isms." Kant's valiant efforts to rescue metaphysics from monistic idealism on one hand and skepticism on the other only made matters worse. The identity between noumena and intellect effected in the act of knowledge had been shattered and, like Humpty-Dumpty, could not be repaired. The balanced realism of Aristotle and Aquinas, dormant for centuries, now lay buried beneath what metaphysical rubble remained after the blast of the Kantian *Critiques*. Unable to abide the German idealists, the scientific spirit of the eighteenth and nineteenth centuries embraced the only alternative left—one or another variety of positivistic materialism. This was the intellectual inheritance of young Freud. He remained faithful to it throughout his life.

15. Jeanniere, *op. cit.*, 11-12.

16. It would be hard to over-estimate the importance of cultural factors in forming individual conscience and influencing behavior. But this is not cultural determinism. On the contrary, we believe that personal freedom is an essential dynamism in the creation, maintenance, and evolution of culture.

17. Applying the laws of thermodynamics to culture, Leslie A. White (*The Science of Culture*, 1950) attributes human progress to the harnessing of energy. The fundamental energy available to man is in himself.

18. "The most fundamental considerations (regarding the social regulation of sex) probably have to do with the consequences of the plasticity, sensitivity, and dependency of the human infant and with certain closely associated features of the place of 'sex' in the need-structures of the human personality." Talcott Parsons, *The Social System* (New York: The Free Press, 1951), 155.

19. We touch here upon a problem that many sociologists and anthropologists would prefer to ignore. There seems to be something in human beings which is attributable neither to culture nor to genetics.

For example, the utterly *arbitrary* use of symbolic sounds which we call language cannot be accounted for by cultural causes, nor can it be explained by human biology. What then does explain it? Scientists readily speak of *abstractions,* but to admit a formal *power of abstraction* in the human mind is too embarrassingly close to admitting the existence of an immaterial intellect.

20. Quoted in L. White, *The Science of Culture* (New York: Grove, 1949), 325.

21. The more complex a society becomes, the more role-functions an individual plays. But a role is a non-emotionally expressive, or "rational," function—direct expression of sexuality is usually impossible and sublimation very difficult. Therefore, as roles multiply, sexual energies have fewer direct outlets of expression—if a satisfactory sublimation is not achieved in these roles, frustration occurs. Mounting frustration causes a build-up of tensions that will seek an outlet in direct expression. And because so few direct expressions of sexuality are available in such a complex society, deviation results. As examples of the two possible extremes, contrast the sex code of an Australian aborigine with that of an American Catholic. The former can commit only one sin: incest. The latter can only do one thing lawfully: "normal" coitus in marriage.

22. J. Fletcher, *Moral Responsibility* (Philadelphia: Westminster Press, 1967), 137.

23. *Ibid.,* 138.

24. If sex does not shape character, how would Fletcher react to this statement of Freud: "What we call the character of the person is built up to a large extent from the material of sexual excitations; it is composed of impulses fixed since infancy and won through sublimation, and of such structures as are destined to suppress effectually those perverse feelings which are recognized as useless. The general perverse sexual disposition of childhood can therefore be esteemed as a source of a number of our virtues, insofar as it incites their creation through the formation of reactions." From *Three Contributions to a Theory of Sex,* Modern Library ed. of *The Basic Writings of Sigmund Freud* (New York: Random House, 1938), 625-626.

25. In the late 1950's and early '60's, Catholic moralists struggled with the problem of demonstrating the "intrinsic" evil in employing such contraceptive techniques as withdrawal, condoms, and diaphragms. Recognizing the improbability of arguments based on the intrinsic biological finality (procreation) of the sex organs, they tried to find arguments that would satisfy the "personalist" dimensions of human sexuality while preserving the traditional moral teaching. Viewing the unobstructed vagina and uterus as symbolic of the wife's "total openness" to her husband, artificial contraception was therefore immoral, because it "closed off" the couple to one another; according to the language of "efficacious signs"

it precluded the intimate and mutual self-giving which ought to be communicated in the marital act.

26. "It would seem appropriate to reiterate a basic theme of this chapter: sex does play an extremely critical role in both the marital and non-marital aspects of our culture. This conclusion is worth repeating, even though it seems patent. The crux of the problem is that eroticism has become an integral part of romantic love, and romantic love is to an increasing degree the basis for male-female relations in premarriage and marriage alike, as well as in extramarital affairs. These considerations . . . make the sexual components of contemporary human relations an issue of vital significance." W. Ehrmann, in *Handbook of Marriage and the Family*, ed. H. T. Christensen (Chicago: Rand McNally, 1964), 612.

CHAPTER FOUR

FANTASY AND ACT

INASMUCH AS OVERT SEXUAL ACTIVITY is necessarily limited for most persons, a far more serious problem is the moral responsibility connected with sexual fantasies. Although many adolescents and adults refrain from masturbation and sexual intercourse, in some cases permanently, no one can avoid sexual fantasies.[1] By sexual fantasies, we mean all daydreams, images, and mental pictures of an erotic nature. These can range from full-blown, orgastic extravaganzas associated with masturbation or sexual intercourse to mild, flitting, amorphous images. Sexual fantasies can be evoked by reading, conversation, a picture, the presence of another person, or may be internally produced, with or without volition. One need only think back over the previous day to realize the number of times that a fantasy or daydream has intruded into the stream of consciousness. Some of them, although not physically arousing, certainly had sexual overtones.

Although the moral judgments concerning overt sexual activities may be very difficult for many people, their uncertainty multiplies in the area of sexual fantasies. Consent is often difficult to assess with respect to acts, but is infinitely more complicated when the focus is on an internal state. The psychological and moral problems that can be caused and aggravated by difficulties with sexual fantasies are particularly acute. Although this can be a problem for a married person, the focus of this chapter is primarily upon the young single person in our culture.

Traditional morality has attempted to deal with sexual fantasies using the model of act morality, that is, grave matter, deliberation, and consent. Inasmuch as the matter is presumed to be almost always grave, this has provoked endless discussion and speculation concerning the consent. The controversy around consent arose because many theologians felt that individuals could not be committing a mortal sin each time they confessed this as a sexual sin. Terms such as *admit*, *entertain*, and *take pleasure in* are defined and interpreted as though they were meaningful guides for the counselor or confessor and the individual. However, the confusion in the mind of the individual person persists, as evidenced by the number of penitents who regularly confess impure thoughts.

One of the difficulties in the traditional theological analysis of sexual fantasies and thoughts has been the terminology. Many definitions use words which can only be understood as having negative connotations, such as *pravis* and *turpis*, roots for words such as "depraved" and "turpitude." This manner of writing can hardly leave the moral theology student with a neutral attitude toward sexuality or erotic fantasies. This usage may be defended on the grounds that these Latin terms are more exactly defined or are traditionally understood, but the psychological impact of these words repeated again and again cannot be far removed from the deplorable "dirty thoughts" in English.

In this area particularly, it is necessary to reaffirm the basic principle that good psychology and good morality cannot be in conflict. In order to establish some realistic moral principles concerning sexual fantasies, it is necessary to have a fairly complete knowledge of the nature of fantasy, its impact on behavior, and the consequences of developing and reinforcing specific attitudes toward fantasies.

NATURE OF FANTASY

The primacy of fantasies (not necessarily sexual) is demonstrated by their occurrence in children long before the capacity for even concrete symbolization is operative. Children of two and three years of age have nightmares, dreams, daydreams, and memory fantasies. Even during the preschool years, one does not have to listen with a theoretical bias to perceive the sexual nature of some fantasies. It is common for children of this age to question the physical differences between the sexes and inevitably to provide some fantastic explanations of their own. Imaginary playmates make their appearance during this phase also, a phenomenon that demands a high degree of active fantasy life.[2]

In adults, fantasy and imagery are normal dimensions of personality and are crucial to successful functioning. Memory most frequently is not of an abstract concept but a picture of the past. A person "sees in his mind's eye" certain situations, actions, or persons from the past, and then translates these into words. These images can be scanned for information and experience relevant to the present, and the person can apply this to the task at hand. We remember, for example, the route we took when we visited someone the last time. We remember that the last time the car sounded like this it needed a tune-up. We can visualize the text or the professor as we prepare for a test.

Daydreams about the future often include fantasies of a better job, more prestige, a bigger home, and so forth and thereby can provide realistic motivation to attain the goal through greater effort. Fantasies are used in the service of reality testing when a person imagines a future event and plans how to handle it, or more or less subconsciously plans an important conversation. An individual can rehearse through fantasy his steps toward a goal and, without the necessity of actual trial and error, reject those means that are not workable.

In adults as well as children, fantasy is a necessary buffer against the complete experience of frustration. Reliving an argument, for instance, can afford relief when a person imagines himself saying the things he should have said. Anyone who has ever attended a boring class or meeting can testify to the relief that fantasy can offer. Imagination is a necessary part of the creative and artistic process and in the average person provides a great part of the experience of joy and happiness. Fantasy is psychologically harmful, of course, when indulged in extensively as an escape, or when it interferes with the necessary activities and functioning of the person.[3]

An essential fact about fantasies is that they can be caused by a need, feeling, or drive, or can act as the stimulus to excite a drive. A common example of the former case occurs when a person is hungry and occasionally catches himself picturing the next meal. As an excitatory stimulus, a vivid fantasy or one that is prolonged and elaborated can elicit the arousal of sexual or aggressive impulses. This will be further discussed in the section on the moral aspects of fantasy.

FANTASY AND BEHAVIOR

The impact of fantasy upon behavior has been the topic of much discussion and research. One vital question is: *to what extent does fantasy provide an outlet for drives, thus reducing the necessity for overt behavioral response, and to what extent does it mirror or even add to overt behavioral responses?* J. L. Singer has summarized some of the pertinent evidence, and although the problem is by no means solved, some conclusions from his research relevant to our concern may be drawn.[4]

The amount of fantasy in the mental life of a person is an aspect of personality functioning that varies greatly among individuals, but is relatively consistent within the person. In other words, some persons have consistently rich fantasy lives while others are relatively impoverished. An individual with a rich fantasy life is generally better able to control the discharge of impulses. The fantasy activity seems to serve as a delay, a buffer between impulse arousal and gratification. Individuals with little experience or practice in fantasy, or those who are actually limited in their introspection, generally react more directly through action to the arousal of impulse or strong feeling. Fantasy-rich persons are at ease with daydreams, capable of using them in the solution of problems, and generally enjoy the fanciful products of their imagination. Those persons who are fantasy-poor are generally more extroverted, task-oriented, and orderly. They also generally are more quick to anger or sexual arousal. To these different kinds of persons, a specific sexual or aggressive fantasy will have differing influences upon behavior. For some it will serve as an indirect, sublimated expression and gratification of sexual impulses. That is, a passing sexual image can be in itself an acknowledgement of sexual attraction, an affirmation of sexuality, and serves as its own satisfaction, not as a stimulus to overt behavioral gratification. For others, a sexual fantasy is a trigger for further elaboration and acts as a stimulus to full sexual arousal.

The attitude that an individual has toward fantasies is also an important determinant of their impact on behavior. If early training has led to an unconscious equation of wish and deed, and if sexual feelings were not tolerated by parents, then the person will experience anxiety at the first appearance of a sexual fantasy. This leads to the necessity for automatic defenses against this possibility of anxiety. What occurs is a preconscious censoring of fantasies and a suppression or immediate rejection of those that do become conscious. Problems necessarily occur when the person begins dating and must acknowledge the role of sexuality in the relationship. Either the anxiety mounts and leads to great repression of sexuality, or sexual impulses tend to overwhelm the person and lead to semi-promiscuous behavior. In either case, there is no establishment of mature controls or a step-by-step modification of inhibitions and behavior. A typical example of the former is an obsessive-compulsive reaction in a religiously-oriented person, commonly called scrupulosity. An example of the other extreme of possible reactions is the person who has not had the opportunity to work through this problem during adolescence because of exceptionally rigid training. When this person reaches twenty-two or twenty-five and becomes deeply involved in a heterosexual relationship for the first time, the controls may not be sufficient, and sexual impulses can be acted out.[5]

Mature psychological adjustment demands a high degree of self-acceptance. This must extend to an acceptance of impulses as a dynamic and constant part of oneself. It is important to note, however, that acceptance of fantasies does not entail plunging into elaborate sexual daydreams or to acting out the fantasies. *There is a great difference between fantasy and act.* The well adjusted person recognizes this difference and is not distraught by fantasies that are not conventional. The person who is anxious over his ability to control impulses is likely to perceive very little gap between fantasy and act and, therefore, to be frightened of the fantasies. Fear of loss of control over impulses is a common sympton among individuals in psychotherapy.[6] The task of psychotherapy is to enable the person to admit these fantasies into consciousness while maintaining control over behavior.

It is impossible to define precisely just what is a normal amount of sexual fantasy. Each individual has a unique combination of life experiences, vividness of imagination, degree of introspection, and interest in his own mental life. However, certain boundaries can be put around the concept of a normal amount of sexual fantasy. For one thing, the brief, flitting sexual images that are triggered by reading, a passing person, or seem to be unrelated to any stimulus are a normal part of the stream of consciousness. The fact that sexuality is an integral dimension of personality makes these fantasies as normal as those that focus on food, money, vocational success, relaxation, and so forth. Sexual fantasies, such as a man's image of an attractive girl nude and a woman's image of a passionate embrace by a man, are common and almost involuntary. Short daydreams about more erotic scenes are also quite normal. It is the extremely rare person who does not naturally have spontaneous sexual fantasies daily. In such a case, there would be a corresponding reduction in all types of fantasies. An excess of sexual fantasies is indicated when the person consistently seeks them out and pursues them to the point of actual sexual arousal, or when they become a preoccupation as contrasted with a diversion.

It is precisely in this allegedly causal relationship between fantasy and act, the presence or absence of a gap, that the moral issue rests. Traditional morality assumes that for all persons there is an inevitable progression from flitting image to welcome fantasy to elaborated daydream to sexual arousal to masturbation or sexual intercourse. It further assumes that if control is weakened in any link of this chain, the entire control system becomes less capable of resisting gratification. Control of sexual behavior, therefore, according to this view, must begin with and concentrate on the first faint stirrings of fantasy. If this is not established, the moral character as a whole is weakened and less able to resist temptation.

Popular guides for an examination of conscience lean heavily on the responsibility of the individual to work constantly at the control of potentially arousing fantasies. This moral position is tenable only if supported by psychological evidence. If man does in fact conform to the behavioral model implicit in the traditional moral position, then the task would be to develop psychologically sound tactics to fortify and reinforce the immediate control of fantasies. If, on the other hand, individuals respond differently to varying intensities and durations of sexual fantasies, or if the evidence shows that rigid, immediate control of fantasy is maladaptive, then the moral position must change accordingly. In fact, the evidence supports the position that too much control is maladaptive.

First, each person has a particular way of reacting to fantasies. In addition to the rough, major dichotomy of fantasy-rich and fantasy-poor persons, there are other important influences on fantasy response. Developmentally, adolescents as a group are more fantasy-prone than children or adults. The degree of cognitive or emotional involvement in external activities also influences the amount and impact of fantasy. An introverted person, for example, who has few demands on his concentration has more time available for fantasy than the thoroughly involved, on-the-go person whose free time is very limited.

Second, what we know about wholesome adjustment does not support automatic rejection of fantasy as in the best interests of the person. Once again, it should be noted that individuals do not relish anxiety- or conflict-producing situations. Therefore, the establishment of a principle of fantasy rejection entails the automatic functioning of suppression or repression. Each fantasy will not be considered on its merits, but indiscriminately rejected. Good adjustment demands that the individual have a minimal capacity to relate to his own fantasy life.[7]

Third, the traditional theology has allowed for only two standards of morality in regard to the licitness of sexual fantasy: one standard proper to the married state and the other proper to the single, celibate state. As with overt behavior, distinctions must be made between the married person, the celibate religious, the young dating person, and the engaged individual in relation to sexual fantasies. For each of these states, a different level of control is demanded. To collapse the very real distinctions between different kinds of non-married persons is to distort their life situations.

INDIVIDUAL RESPONSE TO FANTASY

The first point—that people respond in individual ways to sexual fantasies—is an important fact for counselors and confessors to bear in mind. A confession of "impure thoughts" may very well be for many individuals an unrealistic and unnecessary assumption of wrongdoing. Mere absolution or even encouragement to resist these thoughts can reinforce this attitude of guilt. There is a world of moral difference between the appearance and departure of a fantasy evoked by a pretty girl, and a lengthy, well-constructed daydream in response to pictures in a magazine. The individual must be taught standards of discrimination relevant to himself, or his moral orientation cannot mature in the area of fantasy. A person who is habitually aroused, but does not always masturbate, in response to fantasies created in a situation of solitary contemplation of girlie magazines has a much different problem than a person who experiences sexual fantasies while on a date. Yet both may perceive and confess these as identical "impure thoughts."

A further differential factor among individuals is the amount of fantasy tolerance that the individual has developed. That is, some persons have very little ability to interpose delay between a sexual fantasy and its gratification by masturbation or sexual intercourse. These persons are generally in the fantasy-poor class, tending away from intrapersonal awareness, more accustomed to direct, motor expression of feelings and impulses. Others who enjoy a rich world of available fantasy are generally not as quickly aroused by the same fantasy.

There may be a tendency on the part of counselors and confessors at this point to agree with the fact that people react to fantasies with different levels of delay and control, but to go on and conclude that the best advice for the quickly aroused person is still to avoid or suppress fantasy. This conclusion is wrong. The evidence indicates that individuals should grow into a level of fantasy life that enhances adjustment.

ACCEPTANCE OF FANTASY

In regard to this assertion and the second point discussed earlier, it is worth repeating that a defensive rejection of fantasies does not lead to more moral behavior, but rather to an increasing reliance on defenses to avoid anxiety and moral decisions that the person cannot make with ease. The step to scrupulosity from this position is not a long one. Since fantasies are in-and-out components of conscious life, it demands constant inner vigilance to censor those that are sexual. This can happen only if the individual is very much preoccupied with his fantasy life, always sifting, filtering, accepting, and rejecting fantasies in accord with certain standards, or if he develops an automatic, reflexive policy of indiscriminate rejection and suppression of any fantasy which may have the smallest shadow of a possibility of sexuality. Since the latter alternative is the more economical, expectable way in which man's personality works, it soon happens that even with great conscious effort he cannot admit mild sexual fantasies to awareness without experiencing anxiety or guilt. In addition, if the automatic rejection is reinforced by a conscious perception of moral teachings, the possibility becomes even more remote that this habit can be changed when conditions demand it, for example in marriage.

At what may seem to some as the grave risk of eroding all sexual controls, the person must unlearn the habit of automatic rejection of sexual fantasies. For this, he should be able to substitute a degree of self-awareness and acceptance of normal erotic fantasies with a realistic, accurate evaluation of precisely when a fantasy is becoming morally relevant. This process of change can be aided by counselors and confessors if they can recognize that individual acts or thoughts do not necessarily destroy a moral orientation, especially if the person is seriously attempting to establish realistic controls. To be of any real benefit to a person with a problem in the area of sexual fantasy, a confessor or counselor must have a realistic viewpoint about the moral aspects of fantasy. The critical question in this regard is: *at what point does a sexual fantasy become morally relevant?* Until the psychological evidence is taken into consideration, the moral principles and assertions concerning specific situations will remain too conceptual, too subject to rigid interpretation.

MORAL RELEVANCE OF FANTASIES

The first principle relating to morality and fantasy is that if a sexual fantasy is not a clear and immediate stimulus to arousal, it is not morally relevant. To treat all but the most flitting, involuntary images as proximate occasions of grave sin is to force the individual to draw a moral boundary line too far into the territory of innocuous thoughts. The moral boundary line will vary from person to person, depending on such factors as individual differences in arousal, amount of fantasy life, and the situation. The individual and the confessor or counselor can jointly determine the point at which the person's fantasies generally become arousing. When this has been accomplished, the person is in a position to make responsible moral choices.

In addition, once the standards for acceptance or rejection of fantasy are relatively conscious, they are far more easily modified when the individual achieves a different level of sexual morality, such as engagement or marriage. It is a wholly unreal moral position to assert that a young man or woman on a date, much less an engaged person, is not allowed to have sexual fantasies. The mastery of impulses and feelings cannot, for the mature person, reside in archaic, childhood prohibitions against the wish, but must rest upon a self-conscious awareness of the distinction between wish and deed, and the confidence that behavior can be controlled.

It is important to distinguish between pleasurable enjoyment of a fantasy and sexual arousal. A sexual fantasy can be pleasurably enjoyed without leading to full sexual arousal. The difference is almost always a temporal one. Physical sexual arousal takes time. If a fantasy becomes vivid enough and elaborated, it has become a daydream. And it is an elaborated fantasy or daydream that produces sexual arousal, not a relatively short-lived sexual fantasy. A succession of sexual images does not become morally relevant unless it initiates a process of arousal within the person. Simple pleasurable, even physical enjoyment of a fantasy can occur without full sexual arousal. The individual is still in a position to control the fantasy.

Moral responsibility enters at the point of emotional preoccupation with a fantasy which in turn produces sexual arousal and tension. The control of behavior is dependent upon the decision to suppress a fantasy before it reaches that level of preoccupation. Obviously the person cannot make a responsible moral decision once passions are aroused, and this fact is what led to the traditional ban on the admitting of erotic thoughts and images at their very outset. However, the person can develop a habit of suppressing these fantasies before they reach a critical level of intensity and still allow the normal pleasurable fantasies to be enjoyed. The development of this type of conscious, habitual decision, based on the uniqueness of the person's arousal level and normal fantasy life, prevents the damming up of sexual tension that occurs when fantasies are suppressed or rejected the moment that they appear.

In addition to misconceptions concerning the amount of sexual fantasy that is normal, there are certain mistaken attitudes about the content of these fantasies. Many persons feel that sexual fantasies, if they are normal at all, can only be of adults having intercourse in a face-to-face horizontal position. Any variant of this stereotype is felt to be somehow perverted even in fantasy, let alone act. This attitude, unmodified, can carry over into marriage and destroy the spontaneity and pleasure of a sexual relationship. In reality, sexual deviation is limited to activities in which the object is inappropriate, that is, activities which take the place of sexual intercourse. Generally, if any sexual activity is in the nature of foreplay, serving to arouse desire and ending in sexual intercourse, it is not deviant but normal. Common examples include variations in position and kissing parts of the body other than the mouth. Fantasies of these activities, therefore, are also normal, not evidence of a warped mind.

The above statements should not be interpreted as a blanket endorsement of all kinds of fantasies. As mentioned earlier, fantasies can constitute a significant symptom of psychopathology. In relation to sexual fantasies, there are many opportunities for the intrusion of maladaptive aspects. Singer mentions the relatively common example of elaborated, intensely romanticized fantasies of sexual intercourse in a shy, inhibited person. He points out that the awkward, hesitant first experience of intercourse is so disparate from the fantasy that further withdrawal easily results. Just as likely is the perception of how improbable the realization of the fantasy is and consequent strong resistance to social activity that may bring it about. Other psychologically suspicious fantasies are of the obsessive variety, constantly intruding involuntarily upon consciousness, or the sado-masochistic type in which inflicting or enduring pain is related to sexual pleasure.[8]

The possibility of moral evil arises when a person, knowing his general level of response to fantasy through experience, continues to allow fantasies to cause sexual arousal that leads to gratification through masturbation or sexual intercourse. Once again, the moral evil is paralleled by the psychological damage. Habitual arousal by fantasy and gratification through masturbation are psychologically harmful because of the possibility of a fixation at this immature level. Morally, it is the *habit* that is evil, not the occasional lapse by a person whose orientation is toward responsible sexual adjustment and who is trying to control his behavior. The responsibility of the person lies in either changing the situation so that erotic fantasies are not as likely to occur or, more internally, in a re-evaluation of his perceived threshold of arousal. This must be followed up by a change so that the suppression of fantasies occurs earlier in the person's awareness and enjoyment of them.

FANTASY LEVEL IN DIFFERENT CHASTITY GROUPS

Although the focus of moral precepts relating to fantasy must ultimately be within the individual, certain external group differences need clarification. In particular, there should be a realistically distinct approach to the role of fantasy in different chastity groups. We refer again to the married, the celibate, the dating, and the engaged states. To collapse the differences between the three unmarried states is to impose a monastic-like morality on many persons who are sooner or later to be having intercourse in marriage.

For the married person, sexual fantasies should be encouraged. That is, in the sense that anticipation enhances enjoyment, fantasies can promote sexual pleasure. Obviously, if these fantasies are escapist daydreams of erotic adventures with someone other than the spouse, they can be a source of frustration and hinder the mutuality of sexual pleasure. But generally, sexual fantasies are able to stimulate a sexual relationship and can keep it from becoming dull or mechanical. If sexuality in a marriage is limited to intercourse, it loses its integral character; and it is only a short step to misunderstandings, sexual rejections, or merely physical coupling. It is unfortunate that so many married persons still apply moral standards of the single life to their sexual fantasies. This is most often due to the carry-over of rigid attitudes from the time when they were single and "dirty-thoughts" were a real problem. These individuals generally experience shame or embarrassment in a discussion of sexuality, and consequently the attitudes and behavior do not change. The sexual aspect of the marriage relationship becomes unpleasant or actually distasteful. Since their attitudes are not likely to change, this view of sexuality will be passed on to the children.

In order for a person who has chosen the religious celibate life to maintain control over intrusion of sexual fantasies, it is generally necessary to develop a strong habit of suppression and sublimation. This habit serves a useful purpose in a celibate state of life. It frees the person from the necessity of making decisions each time a fantasy occurs. The danger is that the control will be too stringent or too determined by anxiety. If this develops, the person easily slips into using unconscious censoring and repression, buttressed by attitudes of fear and shame, and adopting the view that anything sexual is impure or dirty.

An integrated, well adjusted use of suppression and sublimation demands a high level of psychosexual development. That is, because the same behavior can reflect many different motives, the use of these mechanisms can be due to anxiety and guilt or to consciously chosen principles. For example, a married man who, immediately before and after his wife gives birth, consciously suppresses sexual fantasies because intercourse is temporarily inadvisable is seeking to avoid the problem of frustrated sexual desire. Contrast this with the unconscious struggle of a celibate person who feels that any sexual thought is a mortal sin and must be constantly vigilant to ward off any possibility of guilt or anxiety. If the training of the person in the novitiate or seminary is based on a repressive view of sexuality, the later control of sexual fantasies will not be under conscious control. Although recent trends in religious formation are encouraging, there is still a strong element of repression and over-control in the area of sexuality.

The fact that sexuality must be more controlled in a celibate person does not entail the automatic rejection of sexual fantasies. The extreme rigidity of control over fantasy advocated by many moralists and priests is in part a result of their own training in which control is held up as an ideal.[9] A self-conscious awareness of his or her own tendency to preoccupation and arousal can help the person to establish a realistic reaction to erotic fantasies. If some of the preoccupation with sexuality is due to unsatisfied curiosity, as is often the case, a partial solution must be knowledge—a straightforward presentation of the facts of life. The moral boundary line for fantasy can then be drawn so that sexual fantasies do not reach the level of a problem, yet do not cause anxiety at the first hint of their appearance. Suppression is a relatively conscious dismissal of fantasies, involving some awareness of the fact that the dismissal is voluntary, and successful suppression depends upon vigilance and effort.

It is unrealistic to insist on the same standards of admissibility of sexual fantasies for persons who are not committed to a celibate way of life. Normal dating and heterosexual social activities will give rise to sexual fantasies. If these cannot be integrated into the individual's moral life as normal occurrences, but rather are perceived as occasions of sin, the consequent anxiety will produce defensive reactions such as attempts at total exclusion of sexual fantasies. Since this is impossible, however, the person will be experiencing "sinful thoughts" much of the time. And because confession usually reinforces the attitude that these fantasies are sinful, the vicious cycle will be established.

The person who is at a dating age, developing an internal norm for judging a prospective spouse, must include the sexual aspect of the relationship in his evaluation of the other. To deny the role of sexuality in a dating relationship, or its impact on attraction, is to ignore the realities of human nature. Equally unrealistic is the position that the normal erotic fantasies of a sexually mature, unmarried person are almost always proximate occasions of sin. If an individual cannot enjoy fantasies that are spontaneously produced by the life situation of dating and heterosexual attraction, he must label them as bad in some way. This can serve to maintain the adolescent separation between personal-affectionate love and sexual love. The person during this stage of his life must have the freedom to work out this area of his moral orientation.

Because the relaxation of the moral boundary line for fantasies must be carried even further for the engaged person, it is during the dating stage that moral reactions to sexual fantasy should become increasingly more realistic. As the person is working out a balance between moral value and impulse gratification, he or she is extremely vulnerable to sin-oriented teachings. One cannot expect an adaptive shift in attitudes at the time of engagement if there was a previous reinforced punitive attitude toward sexual fantasy. It is even more unrealistic to think that a marriage ceremony will change these reactions if they remained fixed during the engagement period. Therefore, from the beginning the individual ought to feel that sexual fantasies are a normal aspect of life and that, like everything else, overindulgence in them can lead to problems.

Moral training should help the individual to recognize his own vulnerabilities as well as his assets in regard to the handling of fantasy. It is the task of the parents, teachers, confessors, and counselors to prevent the formation of an attitude that sexual fantasies are impure or dirty and should be avoided at all costs.

When a person becomes engaged as the result of a mature decision to commit himself to another for life, the deepening of the relationship entails the enjoyment of frankly sexual fantasies. Traditional moral theology recognizes this and imposes no penalty on sexual fantasies at this time because the object is licit. To extrapolate backward, one must ask how is a person to switch from an attitude that sexual fantasies are gravely evil to one that allows their enjoyment overnight or over a month? The answer lies in the modification of controls at the earlier level. This in turn necessitates a relaxation of the teachings, a greater emphasis upon individual differences, and a greater confidence in the conscious control system of the individual.

In the past, the lack of confidence in the ability of the individual to control impulses may well have been justified, for the conscious examination of values by the person may have resulted in their rejection. Now that the social and biological sciences can offer substantiation for the *valid* principles of morality, moralists ought to feel more free to question the basis of a prohibition or to evaluate its impact upon the total functioning of the person.

NOTES TO CHAPTER FOUR

1. L. F. Shaffer and E. J. Shoben, *The Psychology of Adjustment* (2nd ed.; Boston: Houghton-Mifflin, 1956), 205-206; J. L. Singer, *Daydreaming: An Introduction to the Experimental Study of Inner Experience* (New York: Random House, 1966), 57; W. E. Henry, *The Analysis of Fantasy* (New York: Wiley, 1956).

2. S. H. Fraiberg, *The Magic Years* (New York: Scribners, 1959), 15-23.

3. Shaffer and Shoben, *op. cit.*, 200-210.

4. Singer, *op. cit.*

5. The best example of this type of problem is found in those persons who leave the religious life or, prior to leaving, become emotionally involved with a person of the opposite sex. The impact of the relationship is multiplied by the effect of the preceding years of repression of sexual interest and fantasies. The controls in the religious life were never internalized in a mature way, but served as an external pressure to reinforce the almost total denial of legitimate sexual curiosity during the period of life when sexuality should have been integrated with the total personality.

6. K. Colby, *A Primer for Psychotherapists* (New York: Ronald, 1951); R. Ekstein and R. S. Wallerstein, *The Teaching and Learning of Psychotherapy* (New York: Basic Books, 1951).

7. Shaffer and Shoben, *op. cit.*, 200-210; Singer, *op. cit.*, 81-101.

8. Singer, *op. cit.*, 193-214.

9. An example of this attitude toward fantasy is found in Tanquerey's classic on the spiritual life: "In order to check the wanderings of the memory and imagination, we must, first of all, strive to expel from the outset, that is, from the very moment we are aware of them, all *dangerous* fancies and recollections, for such, by conjuring up some crisis of the past, or by carrying us along midst the seductive allurements of the present, or on to those of the future, would constitute for us a source of temptation." A. Tanquerey, *The Spiritual Life* (2nd ed.; Tournai, Belgium: Desclee, 1930), 377.

CHAPTER FIVE

MASTURBATION

As Father John Kirvan of Wayne State University points out in his book *The Restless Believers*, it is usually in a bout with masturbation that the young male Catholic first confronts the challenge of Christianity in a meaningful way.[1] Whether this confrontation is a realistic one, a chance for spiritual and emotional growth, is another question. The problem of masturbation is a real scourge of the Catholic confessional. During the most sensitive years of their lives, the possibility of the "state of grace" for most young people depends—in the estimation of textbook theology and the young people themselves—upon the possibility of their refraining from masturbation. The anomalies connected with this subject are almost too numerous to detail. From scriptural exegesis and classical moral theology to the everyday religion classroom, "examination of conscience" booklets, and confessional experience, the problem is riddled with inconsistencies.

An exhaustive treatment of masturbation is impossible here. We merely intend to offer some insights and suggestions that may permit the reader to steer some kind of middle course in his thinking between the extreme which insists that every act of masturbation is, at least objectively, gravely sinful and the more fashionable approach of some writers today who tend to dismiss the whole matter as inconsequential.

Why is it so often observed in Catholic schools that from about the eighth grade on far fewer boys than girls receive Holy Communion daily? Priests and counselors who regularly deal with adolescents know very well that the physiological and physical differences in the sexes make the objective observance of genital continence much more difficult for boys than for girls. One would hope that most priests hearing the confessions of adolescents take this into account. But our traditional act-centered morality has made it somewhat difficult to appreciate the fact that the diffuse "funny feeling" attendant upon romantic daydreams in a thirteen year old girl is in no way morally different from the phallic urgency accompanying the frankly erotic fantasies of the pubescent young boy. The leniency of many confessors in absolving the young male masturbator is a wholesome consequence of a combination of intuition and experience. One would be hard pressed, however, to find such an important distinction in a standard textbook of moral theology. A certain unconscious dishonesty accounts for many similar differences (and sometimes virtual contradictions) between moral theory and everyday practice.

Although masturbation is a problem encountered during all levels of development,[2] it is particularly acute during adolescence and early adulthood.[3] The resolution or exacerbation of the problem at this age determines if and to what extent masturbation will be a problem later. In regard to moral as well as psychosexual development, an understanding of the major factors operative during adolescence is essential. Therefore, a brief presentation of the major developments during adolescence will serve as an introduction to the problems of moral capacity during adolescence, masturbation in adolescence, and masturbation beyond adolescence.

ADOLESCENCE

Intellectual growth, or cognitive development, is one of the few areas of personality that becomes more stable during adolescence. The attainment of the abstract, conceptual, relational level of thinking (Piaget's level of formal operations) marks the end of sudden or dramatic changes in mental capacity. The research[4] points to a peak in cognitive development occurring between eleven and fourteen years of age, followed by a gradual stabilization. Intelligence tests reflect this fact in several ways: the test items are more abstract at this level; responses are scored for conceptual rather than concrete correctness, and regular tests of adult intelligence are administered to individuals of sixteen years of age.[5]

The youth of fifteen or sixteen is now capable of structuring his thinking about the world along more mature dimensions. He has the capacity to generalize beyond the concrete facts, to deal with abstract and symbolic ideas, to increase his time perspective so as to relate both the past and the future to the present, to evaluate critically his own thoughts and actions as well as those of others, and to reason and judge from principle and value to specific issue or behavior.[6]

The achievement of the capacity for adult sexual functioning is the most obvious development of adolescence. On the average, boys attain physical sexual maturity between 14 and 15 years of age, and for girls, the average age is 13 to 14 years. The important development is not the biological-morphological-physiological changes, but the resulting psychological and social upheaval. Sexual development brings with it many demands for adjustment on the part of the adolescent. The whole area of impulse control is thrown out of the preadolescent equilibrium with the advent of full-blown sexual impulses. The person is faced with feelings and drives that are unfamiliar and powerful, and he or she will spend the next several years working out a balance between gratification of sexual impulses and the demands of moral values.

Of critical importance is the manner in which the sexual drive is psychologically accepted. If the adolescent *could* accept the appearance of erotic fantasies and the physical experience of sexual desires as a normal or even pleasant development, there would not be the necessity for anxiety, shame, guilt, or embarrassment. Experience, however, indicates that sexual maturation often provokes problems that lead to the development of negative feelings toward this aspect of the self.

Socially, adolescence marks an end to activities that are primarily with members of the same sex and of dependence upon parents for guidance, norms, or controls. The adolescent moves into an adult-like role in activities such as parties, group and single dates, and a social milieu that is predominantly peer-oriented and heterosexual. The demands, obviously, are heavy upon the adolescent to adjust to this new social situation with changing rules and high expectations for even more mature behavior. The problem of adjustment is increased by the extreme emotional reactivity of adolescence. All feelings at this time are experienced with more intensity and vividness than before. Disappointments become tragedies, and happiness becomes elation. Mood swings are often abrupt and seemingly unrelated to events. The social result is an alternation of depressed withdrawal and happy involvement.[7]

All these changes in adolescence fragment the previously stable self-concept and feelings of personal identity. The individual must adjust his view of himself to include sexuality, heightened feelings, deeper intellectual understanding, and a vastly broadened social perspective.[8]

MORAL ACTS IN ADOLESCENCE

The implications of these developments for the moral capacity of the adolescent are profound. All the evidence (see notes, Chapter 1, pages 31-33) demonstrates that the *potential* for making moral judgments about long range commitments and orientation is present. The question remains whether this potential can be responsibly actualized by a person in the throes of adolescent adjustment. A definite answer to this question is impossible. However, there are sufficient indications from research to make several assertions.

First, research on the development of moral judgment[9] indicates a great deal of inconsistency and carry-over of childish concepts until about seventeen or eighteen years of age. The sequential nature of moral development and the high correlation between maturity of moral judgment and chronological age would indicate that, prior to this age, moral judgments are determined by and diluted with immaturity and are therefore not completely free.

Second, decisions and judgments in other life areas are demonstrably subject to abrupt reversals, are made impulsively, and are extremely influenced by mood swings. Adolescents of fifteen and sixteen are not taken seriously when they vow everlasting friendship or enmity or when they decide upon a vocation. The common sense experience of adults keeps them from expecting endurance of attitudes or consistency of behavior at this level of development.

It is a safe assumption that during early and middle adolescence (through seventeen or eighteen years of age) moral decisions are neither free nor mature *in a consistent and sustained manner*. Although undoubtedly there are adolescents who achieve moral adulthood before this age, they represent a minority. Adolescents are in a state of transition morally as in other dimensions of personality functioning. Although they have overcome most of the developmental obstacles of childhood morality, they have not as yet achieved a sense of identity, a stabilization of self that maintains continuity and consistency within the personality. Lacking this, it is unreal to assert that adolescents can make valid long range decisions capable of destroying their relationship with God.

We must quickly modify that statement lest it appear that we are seeking to remove all moral responsibility from adolescents younger than eighteen years of age. During the years from approximately thirteen to eighteen years of age, the individual is *becoming* increasingly more aware of his personal relationship with God and more capable of putting habits, attitudes, values, and principles in the perspective of moral orientation. The intervals between these episodes of mature moral judgment become shorter, and the continuity and consistency of the orientation deepen. The adolescent is unquestionably responsible for his behavior. But at this age does the responsibility extend to possible moral shipwreck?

We believe the evidence points to a two-part answer. First, the facts of personality formation force the conclusion that a poor moral orientation begins in childhood and is reinforced in adolescence. Poor habits, attitudes, and values are not likely to be put aside with the coming of full moral maturity, but rather to increase their strength. Therefore, parents and others in authority must continue to make rules and enforce them, rewarding good patterns of behavior and discouraging those that are bad. Because of the continuing responsibility of the parents, that of the adolescent is attenuated. A portion of the youth's obligation is to his own evolving conscience, for there are periods of tentative critical self-evaluation during this time that gradually introduce the person to the level of autonomous self-direction through internalized principles. But in this exploratory phase, the person must test the soundness of his conscience by seeking advice from those who guide him, because the responsibility is still primarily that of obedience to parents. This relationship of responsibility to parents is not *terminal*, as in childhood, but a *mediated* relationship with God. That is, the young adolescent does have a relationship with God, but it is mediated through the parents, because he or she is not yet fully capable of mature moral judgments. In childhood, the relationship with God is not a morally relevant one. The responsibility for moral judgments on the part of the child rests with parents, and in this sense, the child's moral responsibility is terminal with his parents. The second part of our answer is based on this aspect.

The essence of childhood morality is obedience to parents and parent surrogates. Adolescent moral life is essentially one of diminishing obedience and growing autonomy. The adolescent is responsible for the development of good moral habits, in part out of obedience, in part out of a conscious recognition of their long term implications. An adolescent is morally culpable for patterns of behavior which he realizes are a violation of moral values and a threat to his relationship with God. As the integration of moral concepts increases, the responsibility for acting in accord with them increases also. Although an adolescent may not be fully responsible for a particular series of acts because of emotional tension, group pressure, or simple immaturity of control, he is responsible for the modification of his behavior in order to avoid the formation of a bad habit. This responsibility is not to parents, but to his conscience and to God. In this sense, then, an adolescent can slowly shift his moral orientation away from God. He is responsible in a much more proximate way for the habits, attitudes, and values that will crystallize into his adult moral orientation.

To sum up, it is during the early part of adolescence that an individual demonstrates the *potential* for truly moral judgments. Because of the many profound developments occurring in almost all dimensions of personality, it is not until seventeen or eighteen years of age that this capacity can be said to operate in a consistent and sustained manner. During this time, the adolescent's moral responsibility is shifting from a conformity and obedience orientation toward his parents to an adult-like, value-based, autonomous moral orientation involving a relationship with God.

MORAL PERSPECTIVES ON MASTURBATION

A typical argument against masturbation used to be that it was a quasi-destruction of human life, therefore a grievous sin against nature. In the ancient biology the semen was the sole "active principle" of human generation, containing the seed which needed nothing further for its development into the child than to be planted into the body of a female. The woman merely contributed the proper "soil" or environment. Consequently, deliberately to waste the seed of life was to commit a sin similar to the crime of murder. One seminary professor told his class of fourth year theology students that to destroy the sperm was intrinsically evil, because it had the power of self-motility and so had a certain independent life which was, in germ, human life itself. This kind of biologism used to bolster a moral point of view has been repudiated by practically all authors today.

Nor is the puritanical pleasure-is-bad argument going to have much force anymore. People are increasingly being exorcised of the fear of sin in enjoying bodily pleasures. We know from history how profoundly the residues of Manichean dualism affected moral thinking in the West for fourteen centuries. Such was its influence that even a few years ago the Dominican school of moral theology could maintain that every pleasure directly sought for its own sake was at least venially sinful. Implicit in this statement is the principle that pleasure is in itself somehow evil and can only be justified by the goodness of the act which produces it. For example, deliberately to eat a piece of apple pie for the pure pleasure of the taste of cinnamon and fresh apple without at least implicitly intending to be nourished by it would be a venial sin. We may perhaps laugh at the incredible nit-picking of the example, but John Noonan in his

Contraception[10] has painstakingly demonstrated the pervasiveness of this principle throughout the history of the Church's teaching on sex and marriage.

The most serious argument against masturbation and the one currently in general force among Catholic moralists is that based on a version of natural law theory. According to this highly sophisticated philosophy of behavior, human acts are endowed with intrinsic goodness or evil insofar as they objectively promote or thwart the ultimate purpose of man's existence—what Aristotle called beatitude. In further specifying this general principle, however, moral philosophers taught that the sexual organs had a purpose predetermined by their nature (structure and function) which had to be respected by the agent. Not only did this purpose built into the organs demand respect, but it could never be frustrated under any circumstances or for any "higher" reason.[11] For example, a couple might consult a physician for the purpose of conceiving a child. After testing the woman, the gynecologist discovers that she is fertile and the problem is with the husband. Prescinding from the medical utility of male fertility tests, it has been consistently maintained by Catholic moralists that the husband may not masturbate into a sterile container to furnish the laboratory with a suitable semen sample. To consult G. Kelly's *Medico-Moral Problems*[12] is to be astonished at the ingenuity of moralists' attempts to permit the physician to obtain a sample without recourse to direct masturbation. Testicular biopsy, prostatic massage by rectum, perforated condom, Dolle spoon—none of which are medically capable of furnishing the kind of specimen needed for proper laboratory analysis. This is the final reduction to the absurd; because the achieving of orgasm outside of intercourse is held to be *intrinsically* evil (separated from its "natural" purpose) it can never be justified, not even if, theoretically, it were the only possible means of enabling the couple to have a child!

Another instance of the reduction to the absurd of this kind of natural law biologism is the famous controversy in Catholic Canon Law between the Holy Office and the Sacred Roman Rota on the definition of true sexual intercourse.[13] According to Catholic marriage law a marriage must be consummated by an act of sexual intercourse in order to be completely indissoluble. The crux of the question lay in what precisely constituted sexual intercourse. The definition accepted by both parties was that it consisted of three parts: erection and penetration of the vagina on the part of the male, emission of true seed by the male in the vagina, and the retention of the seed by the woman. But what is "true seed"? Supposing a man had his testicles destroyed in battle. He can still perform the act of intercourse and ejaculate, but the ejaculation would not contain spermatazoa. Is such a man capable of a valid marriage?

The arguments, counter-arguments, and solutions are not important for our present purposes. What we feel is important is that the kind of reasoning here, the entire frame of reference, is indicative of a natural law biologism that can no longer support a viable sexual ethic.

MASTURBATION DURING ADOLESCENCE

There is no doubt that masturbation is a problem for most adolescents. The figures[14] show that by twenty years of age over 90 percent of all males and 40 per cent of all females in this country have experienced masturbation. The figures also show that masturbation is not a one-time experiment for most adolescents, but a quickly developed habit. The average frequency of masturbation in young adolescent boys is between two and three times a week. Considering the statistical frequency of masturbation and the nature of the problem itself, several assertions can be made and discussed.

First, masturbation is not an intrinsically evil act. We feel that the question of masturbation must be taken out of the area of "pure" morality and put in the area of psychosexual development to be properly understood. Once the facts have been established, then some worthwhile conclusions relevant to morality may be drawn. Masturbation is, during adolescence, a way of coping with sexual drives and tensions, a form of experimentation, a symptom of adolescence itself. Adolescent masturbation is a "phase-specific sexual activity."[15] It is the bearer of fantasies with which the adolescent must grapple before attempting more mature and adaptive means of heterosexual adjustment. It is morally wrong only when it becomes psychologically harmful. Here, we are not speaking of so-called "compulsive masturbation." This term has been used by moralists for decades to describe what they have erroneously elevated to the status of a problem in itself. There is no such entity as compulsive masturbation. Frequent, habitual masturbation is not a syndrome, but a symptom of another problem. By labeling it "compulsive," the moralists remove both the responsibility for the habit and the motivation to change. Psychologically harmful masturbation is a retardation of psychosexual development, a fixation at the level of autoerotic activity because of anxiety over more mature heterosexual activities. This will be discussed in greater detail in the section on masturbation in adulthood.

Second, masturbation must be seen not as a problem or entity in itself, but *always* as an expression or symptom of some interior psychosexual state. Freud stated, ". . . the problem of masturbation becomes insoluble if we attempt to treat it as a clinical unit, and forget that it can represent the discharge of every variety of sexual component and of every sort of fantasy to which such components give rise."[16] The prevailing layman's thinking seems to be that masturbation is almost universally a substitute for intercourse, always accompanied by heterosexual fantasies. Quite the opposite is true. The nature of the fantasy is far more important than the masturbation, for it reveals which components of the sexual drive are being acted out. Fenichel states that masturbation is certainly pathological in two circumstances: (1) when it is preferred by adults to intercourse, and (2) when it is not done occasionally as a matter of tension reduction, but more frequently for its own sake.[17] The former will be discussed in the next section, while the latter circumstance is the essence of the problem during adolescence, both morally and psychologically.

During the years from the onset of adolescence to about eighteen, occasionally masturbation (with some periods of more frequency and intensity caused by anxiety) *is statistically, psychologically, and morally normal.* This more or less predictable pattern must be seen as developmentally congruent behavior, similar to thumb-sucking or negativism at earlier levels. It is an attempt on the part of an immature organism to cope with a new and therefore threatening constellation of drives, pleasures, prohibitions, and pressures. The extreme to which act-oriented morality has been pushed is exemplified by arguments over the moral licitness of enjoying an orgasm that is the result of a nocturnal emission, a "wet dream." Here, too, the problem is seen as one of pleasure for its own sake being wrong.

As with earlier maladaptive responses, masturbation is abandoned if and when more mature and gratifying behavior is learned. In this regard, the research data provide an invaluable contribution. There is a three-forked road following early adolescent masturbation. One large group moves into direct sexual intercourse, with or without marriage. This group is primarily in the lower social classes. The second large group, the high-school graduate and college level group, maintains or increases the frequency of masturbation, but has a very low frequency of intercourse. A much smaller third group manages to outgrow the phase-specific masturbation of early adolescence and establish controls and sublimations. An interesting reinforcement for the habit theory is the large proportion of the college-educated population who continue to masturbate after marriage.[18]

The moral lesson seems clear. If the adolescent is to outgrow masturbation, he must have an opportunity to develop more mature ways of coping with sexual drives, restrictions, and tension in general. If he is made to feel excessive guilt or shame over this practice, it will tend to fixate the behavior. Punishment, whether external or internal (superego guilt) does not extinguish a habit or form of behavior; it merely suppresses it.[19] Reward and encouragement for different behavior is successful in developing a new habit. In the case of masturbation, as in any other immature reaction, it is far better to appeal to the ego-ideal, the ideal self, rather than the superego to motivate change. That is, if the adolescent can see this practice as inconsistent with his ideal self or his psychological development, change is possible. If, on the other hand, he experiences only guilt and self-condemnation, it is likely that he will develop conflicts and defenses which will work against positive change.

The responsibility of the adolescent between puberty and seventeen or eighteen years of age is to avoid the formation of a habit that is psychologically and morally harmful. Education, counsel, guidance, encouragement, and reward will facilitate the development of better habits. Superego guilt will work against this goal. Parents, teachers, priests, and ministers can do irreparable harm by labeling adolescent masturbation as sinful, impure, or dirty. It can and should be handled as any developmental problem.

Once again it may be necessary to clarify the fact that this point of view does not absolve the adolescent of responsibility. On the contrary, it puts the problem where it belongs, on a relatively conscious, task-oriented basis. An adolescent should feel remorse for acts of masturbation, just as he or she should for indulging in any potentially bad-habit forming activity, such as cheating or reckless driving. But there is a world of difference between conscious remorse or self-reproach and guilt or anxiety over mortally sinful acts. The youth at this age has the responsibility to seek counsel, either from parents, teacher, or priest, in order to avoid the formation of a bad habit. The responsibility also extends to translating helpful advice into behavior. In other words, the adolescent must work on the problem also and see himself as the ultimate agent of change.

In this regard, it is necessary to criticize the recent advent of amateur therapist-priests and ministers who seek to convince the adolescent he is not morally responsible for acts of masturbation, on the assumption that this will relieve guilt. In fact, this only creates anxiety. It implies a force beyond control and destroys motivation to overcome the habit. Almost no one wants to be told that he is not responsible for his actions, even severely disturbed individuals in psychotherapy. If there is no responsibility, there is no subjective possibility of control. The culpability of the adolescent, it is true, does not include the likelihood of condemnation for an act of masturbation. However, the responsibility to try to find a more effective means of dealing with the problem is a serious one, as the development of a bad habit at this age can jeopardize the adolescent's moral and sexual adjustment in adulthood.

Counseling the adolescent who is trying to overcome masturbation demands some knowledge of the fantasies that accompany masturbation. Many times the theme of these fantasies is heterosexual. In these cases, the adolescent often needs to attempt more heterosexually oriented activities, such as parties and group dates, so that actual object relations will take the place of masturbatory fantasies as the means of expressing sexual drives. The fantasies in these instances serve to bridge the gap between the confused sexuality of childhood and mature interpersonal relationships which, in sublimated form, provide sexual gratification.

Masturbation that is accompanied by homosexual fantasies is always a source of anxiety and shame. However, these fantasies do not indicate that the individual is homosexual by any means. Childhood sexuality and early adolescent sexual drives are more amorphous and diffuse than mature sexual impulses. The presence of homosexual fantasies often means that the individual's psychosexual development is inhibited or retarded from moving onto the level of heterosexual object choice. The point in this section is not to advise those who counsel the adolescent how to distinguish normal from abnormal fantasies, but rather to point out the sources of possible anxiety in the adolescent which may be relieved by counseling and which definitely will be exacerbated by feelings of guilt.

The individual who seeks help from a priest or counselor should realize that he has the right to select a person with whom he can discuss his problem easily. He may have to shop around to avoid those who urge solutions such as merely more prayer, or in other ways indirectly aggravate guilt. There are others who will prove unsatisfactory, because they dismiss masturbation from the moral arena. A person can benefit most from a discussion with someone who can ask questions that help the individual to look at his problem from different points of view. Direct advice does not generally help. Many priests and counselors, however, feel bound to give advice or offer concrete recommendations. Discussion can often provide the person with insights into patterns of behavior that he can begin to attempt to change. In this context, confession can be a healing, encouraging experience, rather than a recitation of number and species of sin.

At roughly seventeen or eighteen years of age in our culture there is a developmental landmark. Roughly coincidental with the end of high school is the passage into moral maturity. From this point, the individual is responsible for the direction of his moral orientation. The developmental obstacles have been overcome, and the person is charged with the responsibility for his moral life. During the next few years, the person will consolidate the developmental gains of adolescence and stabilize the elements in his moral orientation. For the single young adult, the most difficult adjustment involves the constellation of forces that dynamically operate in the area of sexuality.

MASTURBATION IN ADULTHOOD

A young man or woman who is dating frequently, but not exclusively with one person, is faced with increased sexual impulses on the one hand and values which forbid direct gratification of these on the other. Often the spurious value of technical virginity, a not-illogical result of insistence upon an act-oriented morality, produces an effect identical morally with the taboo. The person masturbates as a relief from heightened sexual tension that has not been gratified heterosexually. The individual often has the feeling that although masturbation is not good, it is morally preferable to fornication. This attitude is often indirectly reinforced by confessors.

There is some intuitive psychological justification for this position. Granting the strength of sexual drives, the cultural milieu, and the opportunities for excessive stimulation, some gratification is inevitable. Here, a focus upon the orientation rather than the act is more likely to help. If the habit or even infrequent acts are viewed as a discrete entity, very little change is possible. If the act in itself is construed as gravely sinful, even less growth is likely because of the damaging effects of superego guilt. Conscious remorse, however, over an incident that is not congruent with one's moral orientation, self-concept, or ego-ideal can help the person to focus upon tactical, behavior change to reduce the probability of masturbation becoming an entrenched habit.

In the case of the young adult, also, it is just as imperative to view masturbation as a symptom or one of many possible methods of coping with an individual problem. All individuals at a certain age or state in life do not have identical difficulties in sexual adjustment. It is always necessary to consider masturbation as a problem behavior or habit that can represent the discharge of many different components of sexual and aggressive impulses and fantasies. The particular moral relationships between fantasy and act have been discussed in a previous chapter.

Masturbation in marriage is not a problem entity in itself. It must be considered as the same problem in a different context. In married persons as well as single, it can represent many diverse underlying causes. One striking difference, however, is the tendency of confessors to be more lenient with a married person than with a single person who has the same problem of masturbation. This seems to be due to two causes. The first is the traditional two-part morality of sexual conduct: one for the married state, one for the single, celibate state. This attitude implies that since a person is married, and therefore has full sexual privileges, masturbation is indeed wrong, but not as wrong as in the case of a single person who is allowed no direct sexual gratification.

The second cause involves that attitude toward sexual impulses held by some moralists and confessors that exaggerates the strength of these impulses and minimizes the ability of the individual to control them when the gratification is habitual. This view is due partly to ignorance and partly to the repressive training of priests in the area of sexuality. This particular attitude views sexual impulses as so powerful and overwhelming that once undammed, they are rampant and must be satisfied. Therefore, according to this view, a married person who masturbates is succumbing to the necessity of tension reduction. Conversely, the single person must avoid it at all cost, for once control is weakened, it cannot be reestablished or may be only with great difficulty.

Obviously, a single person is more beset with cumulative sexual tension if he resists any overt gratification, for he has no immediate time limit placed upon his continence. For the married person who must abstain from sexual intercourse for a week, a month, or even two or three months in the case of pregnancy, the deprivation is time limited. We are not in this instance referring to cases of prolonged illness or separation, but the average, to-be-expected intervals in every marriage when intercourse is not allowed.

The section above is not meant as an indictment of those married persons who have a masturbation problem. We are rather referring to an unjustified double standard used by a minority of moralists and confessors. The other side of the problem which provides the support for tolerant understanding of masturbation in a married person is the day-to-day presence of a sexual partner, with all the stimulation that can occur without deliberation in that situation. In these cases also, focusing on the orientation rather than the act will produce more long-range good. When masturbation is clearly a direct substitute for sexual intercourse, and when intercourse is not available, the person must distinguish between habitual gratification without attempts to establish control and an occasional, accidental, situation-provoked relief of tension.

In all cases of masturbation in both single and married persons, the best way to aid the person is to examine the habit patterns and circumstances to determine if there may be some unconscious or preconscious "setting up" of the situation. An individual can control events much more effectively when he is aware of his own motives and feelings, even though the awareness may cause some pain to his self-esteem. For example, a single person who is easily aroused by certain magazines or by relatively mild stimulation on dates with a particular person, or a married person who experiences immediate arousal in any intimate situation can take steps to modify their behavior. However, the effectiveness of any change is dependent on the individual's perception of a causal relationship and a willingness to take the necessary steps. If a person does not *always* masturbate in a particular situation, he can convince himself that the stimulus is not the usual cause and despite a firm purpose of amendment can unconsciously sabotage any real change. It is also a frequent situation that the person wants very much to get rid of a masturbation problem, but puts the responsibility on someone else to give him a magical solution or hopes that a strong intention will succeed.

It is wrong for a confessor or counselor to give an individual the impression that prayer and a good intention will conquer the problem. When it does not succeed, the person can only feel more guilty and unworthy, and conclude that there is nothing to be done about the problem. Concentration on the moral orientation rather than the act relieves unnecessary guilt, while concentration on the behavior patterns of the individual can produce effective change.

We cannot insist too frequently upon the principle that it is the pattern of acts, not any particular act in itself, that both determines and manifests personal morality. It is conceivable that a single act can be so intense or uniquely representative of one's inner spiritual orientation that it can be called a mortal sin. But this is very rare in practice. In the case of the masturbator, concentration on the number of individual acts committed or their time frequency can do nothing but harm. The following case, we believe, is typical. A young man has been struggling with a problem of masturbation for several years. He is convinced that he commits a mortal sin each time he indulges in the act. He goes to confession and is "wiped clean." Feeling whole again, he manages to avoid the practice for a week or two. But the old habit almost inevitably reasserts itself. He falls. Now the feelings of guilt, remorse, shame, self-depreciation, and profound discouragement come into play, mobilizing tension and anxiety. He has long been conditioned to release such tension through masturbation. He does so again, and the vicious circle is complete. Masturbation produces guilt which produces anxiety which seeks release in further masturbation.

Marc Oraison says:

> It often happens that a young man of twenty or twenty-two years of age, normal in every sense of the word, who until this time had been enslaved by a habit of masturbation that began in the obscurities of his puberty which nothing in his education had prepared him to cope with, suddenly finds himself liberated from the habit without great effort when he meets a young woman who moves his heart

more than his "flesh." Through this experience he achieves, as in the
discovery of a new world and in a kind of inner liberation, the
possibility of a permanent chastity that he could not previously
attain even with the greatest effort. This is a fact of daily experience
for the psychologist. In such a person the encounter and establishment of this interpersonal dialogue realize the final accomplishment
of his development in a certain harmonization of the different
drives. Now the sexual drive, which hitherto had "gone round in
circles," so to speak, in the absence of the more developed and more
specifically affective drive we have called affection, easily falls into
its proper rhythm and function, thanks to the latter.[20]

Furthermore, it is not at all uncommon for the victim to masturbate several times in close succession, once having "fallen back into
mortal sin."

Perhaps the best question the counselor might ask a person who
has this habit is "are you sincerely trying to do your best to gain
control over sex in your life?" The answer will almost invariably be
an honest "yes." The question embodies several crucial principles.
First, it points up the gradual, developmental nature of attaining
psychosexual maturity, thereby removing the focus upon specific
acts. Second, it diminishes the discouragement, depression, and
anxiety so commonly associated with chronic masturbation by
enabling the penitent to see that everything is not lost by a single
lapse. Third, and perhaps most important, it emphasizes the goal to
be labored for: the eventual ability to control sexual impulses and
use them reasonably. Like every other virtue[21]—whether patience,
prudence, honesty or courage—sexual control is acquired slowly
and painfully. The developmental curve will, hopefully, be upward
—but it cannot help but be irregular.

NOTES TO CHAPTER FIVE

1. J. Kirvan, *The Restless Believers* (Glen Rock, New Jersey: Paulist Press, 1966).

2. S. Fraiberg, *The Magic Years* (New York: Scribner's, 1959); P. Blos, *On Adolescence* (Glencoe, Ill.: Free Press, 1962).

3. A. C. Kinsey, W. B. Pomeroy, and C. E. Martin, *Sexual Behavior in the Human Male* (Philadelphia: Saunders, 1948), 499-510; A. C. Kinsey, W. B. Pomeroy, C. E. Martin, and P. H. Gebhard, *Sexual Behavior in the Human Female* (Philadelphia: Saunders, 1953), 142-148.

4. See the notes in Chapter 1, particularly the work of Flavell, Laurendeau and Pinard, and Sigel.

5. D. Wechsler, *Manual for the Wechsler Adult Intelligence Scale* (New York: Psychological Corp., 1955), 5.

6. Blos, *op. cit.*; L. Kohlberg, "Moral Development and Identification," in *Sixty-Second Yearbook of the National Society for the Study of Education* (Chicago: University of Chicago Press, 1963); J. Piaget, *Judgment and Reasoning in the Child* (New York: Harcourt, Brace, 1928).

7. E. B. Hurlock, *Adolescent Development* (3rd ed.; New York: McGraw-Hill, 1966).

8. E. H. Erikson, *Childhood and Society* (2nd ed.; New York: Norton, 1963).

9. See the notes in Chapter 1, particularly the references to Kohlberg.

10. J. T. Noonan, *Contraception* (Cambridge: Harvard University Press, 1965).

11. As given by one of the most recent and scholarly texts of moral theology (P. M. Zalba, *Theologiae moralis summa*, II [Madrid: Biblioteca de autores cristianos, 1957], 120-165), the sin of "lust" (*luxuria*) is defined as any "inordinate use of the power of generation" (p. 120) and is always both *gravely* sinful (p. 135) and *intrinsically* so (p. 132). The reason is as follows: a human act which contradicts the natural purpose of the action as established by God is intrinsically evil when the first act is not subordinated in the divine scheme to some higher purpose. But the sin of lust is such an act. Therefore. . . .

Regarding the major premise of this syllogism, Zalba points out that every natural act (*actio naturalis*) is, by its nature as constituted by God, ordered to a particular end; e.g., eating is ordered to the nourishment of the body (p. 133). Man commits sin whenever he freely frustrates such built-in purposiveness (*ibid.*).

The use of the generative faculty outside legitimate marriage is sinful, because it is contrary to the procreative intent built into the sexual function by the Creator. Since such a use of sex is *ipso facto disordered*, it is said to be *intrinsically* evil. Furthermore, such a sin is always *gravely* wrong because of the seriousness of subordinating the good of the species to the good of the individual (p. 135). Finally, deliberate use of the sexual faculty outside legitimate marriage is intrinsically and gravely sinful *even if the act is incomplete* (e.g., the case of a man who deliberately stimulates himself to obtain a pleasurable erection, but without intending or obtaining an orgasm) *or merely internal* (e.g., deliberate contemplation of voluptuous thoughts) (*ibid.*).

The difficulties, not to say impossibilities, of reconciling the conceptual approach to sexual morality given above with modern personalist orientations seem insurmountable. This so-called "natural law" argument is too physical and organistic; it defines the human act in terms entirely too narrow and mechanical to be amenable to moral evaluation. As Edward Schillebeeckx remarked in discussing the birth control controversy, "The isolated act cannot always realize to the full all that belongs to a person's basic conviction through an *actus humanus* that lies on a deeper level than the isolated act." (Quoted by F. Bockle in *Moral Problems and Christian Personalism* [Glen Rock, New Jersey: Paulist Press, 1965], 124-125). The morality of an act such as masturbation can only be appreciated in terms of the entire person, not by appealing to some kind of intention inherent in the physiology of an organ. As *Herder's Correspondence* recently pointed out: "The magisterium of the Church should not be as quick as formerly to see in individual rules of behavior which either prevail in society or are laid down by itself, immutable principles of natural law valid for all times and places" (*New Thinking on Natural Law*, IV, [December, 1967], 352).

12. G. Kelly, *Medico-moral Problems* (St. Louis: Catholic Hospital Association, 1958).

13. See the discussion in E. H. Nowlan, "Double Vasectomy and Marital Impotence," *Theological Studies*, VI (1945), 392-427.

14. Kinsey, *op. cit.* (1948), 502; Kinsey, *op. cit.* (1953), 142.

15. Blos, *op. cit.*, 160.

16. S. Freud, "A Case of Obsessional Neurosis," in *Standard Edition of the Works of Sigmund Freud*, quoted in Blos, *op. cit.*

17. O. Fenichel, *The Psychoanalytic Theory of Neurosis* (New York: Norton, 1945), 76.

18. Kinsey, *op. cit.* (1948), 500 ff.

19. E. R. Hilgard and R. C. Atkinson, *Introduction to Psychology* (New York: Harcourt, Brace, 1967), 356-359.

20. M. Oraison, *Illusion and Anxiety* (New York: Macmillan, 1963), 111.

21. "Theoretically speaking, from the point of view of psycho-emotional development, sexual relations that do not engage the whole person—that is to say the totality of life—are only incomplete attempts (at shaking off an emotional egocentricity), implying a basic refusal to give and tending to imprison the subject in the compromise state of an adolescence from which there is no exit" (Oraison, *op. cit.*, 110).

CHAPTER SIX

PREMARITAL SEXUALITY

THE LONGSTANDING PROBLEM of premarital sexuality, far from
diminishing, will probably continue to grow. For one reason, the
period of adolescence is lengthening. The amount of time between
sexual maturation and the completion of necessary education and
training is being increasingly extended as more and more individuals remain in school for more years. It is true that the average age
for marriage has decreased steadily during the past thirty years, but
there is a larger number of persons who are and will be going
through adolescence. Another factor is the milieu in which the single person is forced to work out a balance between sexual impulses
and moral principles and values. The adolescent or young adult
today is assaulted with overt sexuality in advertising and entertain-
ment, and finds it increasingly difficult to resist what must appear
to be a near-universal preoccupation with erotic fantasies and sexual
activity. The conflict between what a person believes to be morally
right and what he or she experiences as strong, almost irresistible
impulses is a poignant one.

We certainly object to the idea that sexual sins are the most
"immoral" sins a man can commit; nevertheless, we have to remember that for everyone sexuality is the most important, the most
personal aspect of life that impinges upon their relationship with
God. We make a mistake to equate sex with sheer lust or love.
There is much more to it. Hardly a single virtue is not or cannot be
a sublimation of the sex drive. Conversely, hardly a single vice
cannot find its most intense expression in a sexual outlet. We know

121

from psychological research how commonly sex is bound up with hostility and aggression.[1] Sex can be used to assert domination over another, to show contempt for another. In its ideal context, sex can be the expression of the highest love of which man is capable. In the truly Christian marriage, the marital love of the couple is charity—love for God himself.

There is certainly a crisis in morality today, particularly a revolution in sexual morals. This revolution focuses especially on the young people—those under thirty years of age. These young men and women are not lacking in moral sensitivity or unwilling to do what is right. Perhaps we have betrayed them. We have continued to teach the taboos of our society, continued to teach the do's and dont's, but we have neglected for a long time (perhaps we have even forgotten) the reasons behind the moral maxims and conclusions that we can so blithely hand down to them in the name of wisdom.

Taboos are to be found in every society, and they are a very essential complement to personal experience. Moreover, they are necessary for the smooth functioning of society. They embody—often in ritualized or other non-rational forms—the cumulative wisdom of past generations. One of the most important reasons for the crisis we are experiencing today is that the taboos of our culture have come under ruthless questioning and criticism to the point of being largely destroyed. The struts are knocked out from beneath us. It is too much to expect that today's students and young adults will continue to act upon the patterns of moral behavior handed down by parents, teachers, and religious counselors without reasons or adequate motivation. They are faced with the problem (and it is enormous) of trying to rediscover *why* certain kinds of behavior are wrong. The concept of something being *intrinsically* evil (bad in such a way that it can never, under any circumstances, be justified) has long been abandoned outside the Churches and today is being criticized and rejected even by a growing number of Roman Catholic theologians. A relativist world-view has been substituted for an absolute one in the physical sciences. A dynamic, processive, existentialist philosophy dominates the humanities and behavioral sciences. Is it any wonder that any attempt today to base an ethic upon static, absolutist concepts not only fails to motivate people, but cannot even be understood?

Why is adultery wrong? Granted that it is usually and in principle harmful, is it conceivable that under certain strictly limited circumstances it might be justified or at least tolerated? Such is the kind of question being raised by the increasingly popular "New Morality." Why is premarital experimentation or the manifestation of sexual love in a non-marital context wrong? Where is the harm? It is useless and naive to appeal to the law of God. God is not a despot who makes laws for the selfish satisfaction of being obeyed. If God forbids something, it is the task of theology to show why it is forbidden, how it is harmful to the real good of the person. Is there not a significant difference between Tom and Rita who find each other exciting and indulge each other sexually on their third date and similar behavior between Paul and Sally who are engaged to be married?

We have taboos against homosexuality. We have taboos against divorce, against contraception, against abortion, against pre-marital "petting" and intercourse, against masturbation, against "impure" thoughts. But there is considerable justification for thinking that the classical reasons why these things are wrong—why these sins are sins—are either inadequate or invalid. They are at the very least incapable of motivating young adults to adhere to the traditional codes of morality we have long considered to be of the perennial essence of Christian moral conduct.

INADEQUACY OF TABOO MORALITY

In order for moral choice in sexual situations to be in accord with principles, these principles and values must be a well-integrated part of the personality. *Integration is impossible if the person does not or cannot understand the reasons underlying the principles of conduct.* Although apparently "moral" behavior can occur in the absence of this understanding, it is not a free, human act if it is psychologically determined by a punitive, archaic, childish conscience. Similarly, a lack of understanding makes it extremely difficult for a person to defend himself against arguments supporting sexual freedom. It is difficult to resist the argument that "Everyone is doing it."

Premarital intercourse is indeed a common phenomenon. According to the research on sexual behavior and attitudes,[2] during the period of 16 to 25 years of age, between 64 per cent and 90 per cent of single males experience intercourse. For single females the figures are between 20 per cent and 50 per cent. Although moral reasons are by far those most frequently given for continence, this may be cause for concern rather than satisfaction. Because as more and more adolescents and young adults develop a critically questioning attitude toward moral principles, those that are not rationally substantiated may be rejected.

Take the question of fornication. It is interesting to read St. Thomas' reasons for the immorality of this, the "least serious of the complete sins against chastity." It is surprising how simply pragmatic Aquinas is in his treatment of this sin. He rests his case essentially upon the injustice done to the potential child who has a right to be raised in the stable, loving environment of two parents and the consequent injustice done to society if it should have to bear the burden of rearing the child in the absence of the parents.[3]

Modern contraceptives can all but eliminate the serious possibility of pregnancy occurring as a result of sexual intercourse. In the case of two sterile persons or where there is no significant possibility of a child resulting from sexual intercourse wherein lies the sin? The rigorously logical approach of Aquinas lists masturbation as a more grievous sin than fornication; for masturbation is "against nature," while fornication is "according to nature." We completely reverse this hierarchy in our modern thinking. How do we justify it?

We are not necessarily disagreeing with the conclusions of the older morality about these issues. But we do want to emphasize again that we are convinced that the reasons adduced are wholly insufficient to give individuals the motivation necessary to maintain a moral course of action in their sexual lives. We must realize that the sexual life of a human being is not something to be divorced from the total context of his life. As mentioned earlier, human sexuality is capable of manifesting all of the virtues and all of the vices. Freud is not entirely wrong in his emphasis upon sexuality as the root of neurosis and the solution of sexual conflicts as requisite for the maintenance of psychic well-being.

The taboo morality of the past is wholly inadequate to meet the needs of today's young adults. Not that the taboos are necessarily wrong; it is simply that they do not realistically exist for people today. To tell a young man that he must not pet on a date because it displeases God is simply to frustrate him and undermine the very thing that the moral code is trying to reinforce. Most young people want to do what is right, but they need to see that what they are asked to do is something which is positively able to contribute to their happiness and welfare. They refuse to be the subjects of a "system" or any form of authoritarian manipulation. They will defy any attempt to make them the victims (as they see it) of a joyless code of restrictions they had no part in making and which they could only keep with incredible difficulty in the absence of a more positive, personalist motivation.

The first thing that ought to be explained is that human moral behavior can never be reduced to black-or-white categories. One cannot expect the kind of reasoning used in mathematics and the physical sciences to demonstrate the principles and conclusions of ethics. Ethics and morality are concerned with values, goals, attitudinal orientations—none of which can be successfully reduced to the univocal terminology and syllogistically arranged quantifications of the mathematical sciences. Human nature is too complex, the social dimensions are too profound to expect naive and facile solutions to these perennial problems of human behavior. Ethics has not in the past been immune to the influence of mathematic-like methodology. People have been given the impression that definite conclusions have universal binding power, admitting of no exception. In an area such as ethics, one cannot have this kind of certitude. It is our approach throughout this book to defend a particular moral stance or conclusion not by appeal to authority (whether that authority be Scripture or the teaching of theologians), but by attempting to show the real good fostered or the real harm done to the human person, either in his concrete individual life or in the context of the culture in which he finds himself.

Are there any good reasons why single persons should delay sexual intercourse until marriage? We feel that there are some strong reasons in favor of premarital continence, but that there are also some reasons against it that need to be discussed and analyzed, not merely dismissed.

ARGUMENTS SUPPORTING PREMARITAL INTERCOURSE

To begin with the negative arguments, it is often asserted that premarital intercourse is natural and normal. This argument rests primarily upon the long interval between sexual maturation and marriage in our culture. Those who advance this argument state that continence imposes an unnatural strain, considering the strength of drives and the natural role that sexuality plays in a relationship between a young man and woman. Cross-cultural studies do show that our society (the Judeo-Christian Western Culture) is one of the few that does not condone premarital intercourse.[4]

Closely tied to this is the relatively recent argument that repression and inhibition of normal sexual impulses are not only unnatural, but psychologically harmful. The support for this position is the evidence from psychopathology and psychotherapy concerning the negative effects on interpersonal (including sexual) behavior due to deep-seated conflicts, repressions, anxiety, and guilt over sexual attitudes and behavior that were generated by strict, authoritarian superego sanctions.

A third argument is based on the evidence accumulated to date that indicates that sexual adjustment is one of the most difficult areas of adjustment at the beginning of a marriage.[5] The facts do show that sexual inhibitions, attitudes of disgust, and frigidity or impotence in marriage can result from long-standing avoidance of premarital sexual contact, buttressed by powerful conflicts and defenses. Even less serious problems such as mild shame, embarrassment or excessive modesty can effectively disrupt sexual adjustment in a marriage. An individual cannot maintain attitudes and behavior in accord with the principle of premarital continence for several years and then expect them to be erased by a ceremony immediately preceding the first experience with complete sexual behavior.

There are several responses to these arguments that do not depend on religious or moral tradition. In response to the assertion that the strength of sexual impulses and the natural role of sexuality in relationships preclude sexual continence, one may ask for evidence. That is, do those who do not engage in premarital intercourse (the minority of respondents in Kinsey's survey) exhibit significantly more problems in sexual control, interpersonal relations, symptomatic behavior, and so forth? *Or is it possible that this control can be an integral aspect of mature ego functioning?*

This question leads to the next argument concerning the psychological hazards inherent in repression of normal sexual impulses. It must be made clear that this is a distortion of Freud's position, as well as that of later authorities. Freud, who is often referred to as justification for this position, indeed demonstrated the maladaptive behavior that can result from repression. However, there is an enormous difference between repression motivated by unconscious conflicts on the one hand, and conscious control and sublimation of impulses on the other. Repression is caused by a pre-existing neurotic disorder. Conscious control, employing suppression and sublimation, is an integral part of adult functioning. It is not limited to the area of sexuality, but deals with other impulses, such as aggression, which can be aroused by many situations. Freud, later psychoanalytic writers, and current authorities[6] stress the necessity of integrated conscious control and the value of sublimation, rather than advocating immediate impulse gratification. Freud defined maturity as the capacity to delay gratification. For more than moral reasons, society insists on control of sexual impulses. Norman Cameron states:

> It is as necessary as ever, in the interest of peaceful coexistence and social stability, to restrict direct sexual expression and satisfaction among adults to certain well-defined, institutionalized relationships.

The alternative is to invite open conflict among adults with respect to the rights and limitations involved in sexual possession and parenthood.[7]

A more challenging argument is the positive relationship between premarital sexual experience and sexual adjustment in marriage. Dr. Kinsey,[8] using frequency of orgasm during the early part of a marriage as one index of sexual adjustment, concluded that the evidence was very strong; successful premarital intercourse was very highly correlated with frequency of orgasm in marriage. One is hard put to dispute a maxim as strong as practice makes perfect. Similarly, a study by J. T. Landis[9] showed that only 52 percent of married couples reported a satisfactory sexual adjustment from the beginning of their marriage. Authorities[10] generally agree that although the sexual area is not the most important aspect of marital adjustment, it is many times the most difficult.

Several things can be said in response to this point. In regard to Landis' study, the majority of couples (77 percent) reported that satisfactory sexual adjustment was attained between one month and one year from the beginning of the marriage. Kinsey's figures are not directly comparable; however, he emphasized that orgasm is not the most important criterion of sexual adjustment, but is secondary to the affectionate relationship and general adjustment of the couple.

There are without question problems of sexual adjustment encountered in any marriage, just as there are problems of adjustment in areas such as money matters, in-laws, and parenthood. It would be a mistake, however, to view premarital continence as the sole, or even the most important, cause of problems in sexual adjustment in marriage. More realistically, the cause lies in the entire constellation of habits and attitudes that the single person develops as a result of early experiences, family attitudes, education, and moral and religious training. Certainly moral training that focusses on the evil of specific sexual acts must cause unnecessary conflict and anxiety over later physical contact. For the individual to behave morally and to operate efficiently, he *must* build up attitudes and defenses toward physical contact that make it possible to avoid the constant arousal of impulses, conflict, anxiety, and guilt. The simplest way is the development of an attitude that all sexual activity is wrong. Constant reinforcement of this attitude comes from both avoiding temptation (positive reinforcement) and succumbing to impulses which in turn produces excessive guilt (negative reinforcement). Several years of this unquestioning acceptance of moral standards and suppression of impulse will produce strong inhibitions and anxiety that will interfere with normal sexual behavior.

The solution to this very real problem does not lie in glib suggestions for premarital experimentation and practice. For persons who place some value on principles of premarital continence, this would provoke severe guilt reactions. The answer, unfortunately, is neither easy nor swift. It must begin with wholesome childhood training in the home, open communication with parents about sexual matters, realistic moral and religious education, and the resulting total moral orientation of the person. A wholesome moral orientation rests upon sound reasons for moral principles, such as premarital continence, and upon acceptance of the place of sexuality in relationships.

There are, we feel, sound reasons that support the traditional ban on premarital sexuality. If understood, these can be of great help to those who feel that there is some validity to the principles, but who are not impressed by traditional arguments mustered in support of these principles.

ARGUMENTS SUPPORTING PREMARITAL CONTINENCE

One reason for premarital continence rests on the nature of a mature relationship and the dimensions of fidelity. It is important that the place of sexuality in a relationship be defined. Heterosexual attraction plays a decisive role in dating, courtship, and social activities among the unmarried. But an important fact is that mature sexuality, as it is manifested through sexual intercourse, is an expression, a culmination of the total interpersonal relationship. Sex is not the cause or the sustaining power of a mature relationship. *Only love built up apart from sex can be expressed sexually.* Sexual activity that is not founded upon a close relationship is exploitation or mere tension reduction.

Casual sexual relationships almost invariably lead to an unstructuring of certain ego functions necessary for mature interpersonal relationships. In the critical area of impulse control a deficit in ability to control sexual impulses would have repercussions on the handling of other impulses. Recent research in this area[11] documents its negative effects upon heterosexual relationships in general, close intimate relationships, attitudes of trust, and other basic feelings necessary for mature interpersonal relationships.

Most single young adults, however, do not consider themselves promiscuous. If a couple is involved in sexual relationships, they do not consider it fleeting or casual, but as reflecting a commitment. It is important in this regard to assert that a total dedication to another person cannot be genuine if it is but one of several such commitments made over a two or three year span. Genuine commitments based on a total relationship cannot be made and withdrawn in a matter of weeks. If this occurs, some of the effects of promiscuity will be evident in the personality.

Let us investigate what is implied by a full commitment to another person. Sexuality by its very nature demands a certain *exclusiveness, possessiveness,* and *permanence.* These qualities are desired and, to some degree at least, present in every genuine sexual relationship. We can easily exclude the case of two people who are consciously exploiting each other in their mutual sexual indulgence. Such actions are almost universally recognized to be selfish, therefore wrong. Most cases involve two people who are, at least ostensibly, sincere about their love for one another and their desire to marry. They cannot define love—they are not even sure that "love" exists in their relationship. (Young adults are extremely skeptical about what constitutes "love"—they have few delusions about traditional romanticism in marriage. They seem willing to accept a certain tentativeness in their relationship, even when that relationship is sealed by the marriage vows.) But they are genuinely concerned about each other. What is the meaning of sex in their relationship? Sex is certainly something that cannot be lightly indulged without serious consequences. Once a boy begins to feel a special affection for a girl, the erotic element enters the picture. Immediately the person toward whom this eroticism is directed becomes singled out for a certain exclusive and possessive relationship. Other female acquaintances he may have are no longer on the same level. Consider the love songs of our culture, the poems, the popular music—in every man's heart there is a desire for the endurance, even the "eternity," of this love. We cannot do much about the way we are made. There are strong reasons for believing that when a given sexual relationship contains the elements of exclusivity, possessiveness (without jealousy), and permanence it will bring happiness. Where one of these elements is missing or uncertain, it will engender destructive tension and unhappiness.

Everybody at least theoretically admits the importance of love in the sexual relationship. Without love sex can only too easily express or become the vehicle for the expression of the violent elements never too far below the surface of human nature. Sex with love is ennobling and uplifting. There is perhaps no better definition of love than that given by St. Thomas Aquinas when he says that the highest love is that which wills the good of the beloved as though it were one's own. An identity of wills—this is the real essence of love. It implies that one knows what is the true good of the other and that one works for that good (not simply wishes it) as though it were one's own.

That is no easy task. The essence of love is present, hopefully, in the beginning of marriage, but its full fruition is the work of years. It is perhaps impossible to expect that young couples should be able to love with no admixture of selfishness. As the incidence of character or personality immaturity increases in our culture, so does the commonness of narcissism in marriage.

In the ordinary premarital sexual affair, there is no way of distinguishing whether the love that is expressed is the kind of serious intent to serve the other upon which a marriage must be based, or whether it is purely selfish. Probably it will be a combination of both. But what is crucial is that 1) the self-love present in the relationship be subordinate to the couples' demonstrated desire to dedicate themselves to one another's best welfare, and 2) that the rudimentary ability to carry out this dedication has already been convincingly demonstrated during the courtship period. We believe that, far from making it possible for two people to know each other better or to increase their love for each other, premarital sexual activity diminishes or destroys the capacity to make a reasonable judgment concerning the viability of the relationship, removes the possibility of establishing by deeds—not simply words —that love is paramount, and destroys or seriously impairs the possibility of establishing a foundation of trust for the future. Let us take these points one at a time.

DIMENSIONS OF FIDELITY

Fidelity and the unquestioned trust of each spouse in the other's commitment to be faithful are necessary conditions of a happy marriage. It is interesting in this connection to note that in the Catholic Church adultery is the only crime which need not be forgiven by the innocent party *even if the guilty party is truly penitent.* The reason given by moralists and canonists is that adultery strikes an axe-blow at the very substance of marriage: fidelity. It is simply the case that it is not possible for a person to give himself totally to two people at once. Sexual love is a total sharing of two personalities to a greater or lesser degree. The greater the degree of sharing or the deeper the communication, the stronger is the love and happiness. A man can share many things with others, but no man can share his wife with another (barring extreme depravity). Bishop Fulton Sheen used to quip in this connection that two people can totally possess the same idea, but two people cannot both eat the same piece of pie. What he meant was that the love characteristic of intellectual and spiritual friendships can be shared by many people simultaneously. You can have fourteen good friends, and each of those friendships can be deeply intense and unique. But the kind of friendship that sexual love implies is much more than a sharing of feelings, ideas, goals, work, etc. Only in sexual love is the fullest sharing of total person with total person possible. This is both the agony and the ecstasy of sex.

The capability of sexual love and response is a delicate mechanism easily damaged or destroyed. Sex is not the orgasm. Sex is the uniquely human power of so relating to another human person that the result of the relationship is two persons becoming one flesh. Sexual union is such a total human act that if used irresponsibly it can lead to cynicism, frigidity, desensitization to other human values and emotions. Ultimately it can result in the supreme tragedy of dooming a person to life-long unhappiness—the inability to love at all.

If sexual union is truly the sharing of one's whole person with another, it seems to follow that there are definite limits to the number of persons with whom one can share one's whole self. As a matter of fact, it can only genuinely happen with one person—it can only happen in what we call marriage. Isn't the boy who says to his girl as he has intercourse with her "I love you with all of me, I give you my self" in some danger of becoming chronically insensitive if he later has intercourse with others? For every act of sexual intercourse means precisely that—a giving of the whole self. How does one honestly give himself completely to one person, take himself back, and then give himself to another? This is certainly a common enough fact. But we must observe here that those who engage in multiple sexual experiences *do not in fact intend to give themselves wholly to the partner.* Whether we choose to like it or not, sexuality is a precise and delicate instrument meant for communion of two persons in love. Used otherwise, it must inevitably become blunted—even destroyed.

Almost everyone would agree that sex is right only for two people who are in love. How is this determined? Young people freely admit that when a particular amorous affair breaks up, they were only infatuated. It is more difficult for them to see that while in retrospect it might have been only an infatuation, at the time it was going on it was "love." What *is* love? It seems almost a given in these matters that love and infatuation can be distinguished only in retrospect if emotions alone are the criteria of judgment.

As far as emotional intensity and involvement are concerned, it usually comes as a shock to a young couple in love to be told that each of them can be expected to fall in love with another than their spouse several times after marriage. They frankly don't believe it. Given the usual imprudences of which practically everyone is guilty, the seductive and sex-saturated culture we live in, the close proximity of the sexes without the cultural guards that formerly existed, falling in love with somebody else after marriage is to be expected as a matter of course. And yet fidelity remains essential to marriage. How does a young couple establish their trust in each other's fidelity? Isn't there something that must distinguish the kind of love that forms the basis for a lasting marriage from the kind of love which the all too frequent incidence of adultery typifies? Is there some test by which one can know that the sexual attraction he feels for his beloved is really an *expression* and *not the substance* of his love for her? It is absolutely necessary for two people to prove to each other by their actions (since talk is cheap) that their sexual need for one another is really subordinate to their love. If a young man says, in effect, "I love you therefore I must have you," he is saying very convincingly that he cannot or does not distinguish love from sex. If he cannot demonstrate his love for his fiancee by forgoing its genital expression now, will he ever be able to do so later on in marriage?

Every good has its price. The greater the goal, the higher the achievement, the more it costs in terms of personal sacrifice. A happy, stable marriage is one of the greatest goods possible. It is not a material good that can be purchased in dollars. It is a complex good of the highest emotional and spiritual order. Its price is exacted in the coin of profound emotional and spiritual investment. The couple in love must realize, first of all, that sexual acts between them are the expression of their relationship, not its cause. Only that degree of love which has been built up outside of sex can be expressed in sex. Premature sexual acts can "short-circuit" the full development of love. Conjugal love is multidimensional—it includes tenderness, affection, intellectual communality, sensitivity, and sacrifice. All these aspects and more constitute the kind of total love which marriage must be. Sex in marriage will express these dimensions of love. But a couple must know that they are present in their relationship before they decide to marry. Premature sex acts will so confuse the issue that the couple will not be able to distinguish love from its expression.

We come now to a certain painful paradox: before marriage a couple must grow in their love for each other in a physical as well as psychological way, but they must not have intercourse. This will result in considerable tension. *This tension, far from being harmful, is the most important element in the development of sexual love.* It must not be avoided—it should be anticipated and even encouraged. Tension, contrary to some popular misconceptions, is not a bad thing. Some tensions are creative. To eliminate all tension is to eliminate all human striving, growth, and accomplishment. We want to say that the tension resulting from the denial of complete sexual gratification before marriage is the only effective means of establishing the foundation of mutual trust essential to the future of the marriage and also of forcing the love relationship to expand itself into all the other dimensions mentioned above.

Let's take a case from life. It is selected not because it is interesting or exceptional, but because it is so typical of hundreds of similar cases dealt with in ordinary marriage counseling.

John and Mary were married at the ages of 20 and 19 respectively. They had been having relations regularly before marriage until Mary got pregnant. John had only a high school education, so he decided to go to night school four times a week to become an electrician. They were "deeply in love." He was a quiet, steady fellow who worked days in an auto plant. Mary stayed home, planning each evening's supper with great care. Pregnancy in her case had kept her somewhat ill, but after the baby was born she felt well and became extremely bored at home. One year after marriage she talked John into letting her get a part-time job working midnights at a local factory. He had noticed that she had become increasingly cool toward him sexually, but he attributed it to his own tiredness and her resentment at his being home so little of the time. He thought it would be good for both of them if she worked a few hours a week. Three months after she began working, she broke the news to him. She no longer loved him, was seeing another man and having relations with him. She wanted a divorce.

The counseling interview opened up an ordinary etiology of the breakdown of their marriage. Mary confessed that for a long time she had felt sexually neglected by John. She suspected that he was attracted to someone else, because before marriage he had always been so ardent and insatiable. She felt guilty for thinking that way about him and never mentioned her suspicion. Gradually she became colder in sex with him, while arguments about peripheral matters grew more frequent. She encouraged the advances of a male worker at the shop, because she "needed to mean something to someone."

As a matter of fact, John had never been unfaithful to Mary, but there was no way he could prove it to her. It would not have mattered anyway, since by now whatever love she once might have felt for him was gone. They obtained a divorce.

Counseling was unsuccessful in this marriage not only because the problem was recognized too late to be helped, but also because there was little if any real foundation of genuine love upon which to rebuild the relationship. Their premarital relationship had never cost either of them anything. They did not know the meaning of self-sacrifice. They were wholly unable to distinguish the *feeling* of being in love from the *commitment* to love.

Feelings come and go in every marriage. What the vows of marriage do is stabilize and make permanent a conjugal relationship by lifting it above the whims and vicissitudes of feeling. But no couple can responsibly speak the vows of marriage without some concrete evidence that their relationship is truly a commitment beyond mere need or feeling. And, we will argue, that evidence can only be supplied by the concomitance of two factors in the courtship period: *sexual need* for one another as the only full expression of the love experienced plus the deliberate and meaningful *mutually agreed upon sacrifice* of that expression of love until marriage.

Terribly old fashioned! Perhaps, in a certain sense. Yet the evidence seems to indicate that the traditional prohibition of premarital sex experience might have been very right, but for wrong or inadequate reasons. It may seem a little too hardheaded, but it is another fact of human nature that if two people can rationalize sexual intercourse with one another before marriage, against the commonly accepted code of most religions and civil society on the grounds that they "love each other," no vows pronounced before a minister or magistrate in ten minutes are going to eliminate similar rationalizations for adultery after marriage. The big question keeps coming up: If a couple does not demonstrate impulse control before marriage, what assurance will they have of this control after marriage? Again, if the relationship cost the person nothing before marriage, how does he know it will be worth anything after marriage? If he could not, demonstrably, do without sex before marriage, how will he do without it after marriage? (Let's note that in every marriage at some time or other sexual intercourse is not possible or advisable for lengthy periods of time.)

Given a healthy, loving marriage, it seems that such normal problems as sickness, financial difficulties, in-law problems would not tear that marriage apart. Faced with such obstacles, a happy couple would come more closely together in trying to work out a reasonable solution. But if there is a latent suspicion, a latent and usually unconscious hostility in the marriage, such external problems might well be the immediate cause of marriage failure. That is the anomaly of the statistics which allege that the primary cause of divorce is financial difficulties, second only to in-law problems. This is absurd. The alleged "causes" are not truly causative of the marriage failure. They are hammer-blows upon a piece of rock that is already cracked. And that crack is, more often than not, a profound and usually unconscious lack of trust in the depth of the love relationship which is marriage. That is why the primary need for couples in love is to establish a trust in one another's love so solidly that it cannot be shaken by the ordinary difficulties and temptations that assail every marriage.

A couple must avoid sexual intercourse before marriage. But how can they express their relationship to each other if they are limited to mere words? The unique and essential characteristic of marital love is that it is "body-person" love. A couple before marriage have to grow in their love for each other physically as well as psychologically. The harm of a "don't touch me" puritanism lies in its tendency to divorce the physical side of love from its emotional and spiritual aspects. This leads us to the question of the moral and psychological problem of "petting."

The usual teaching of moral theology regarding sexual touches outside of marriage is that they are always forbidden. Deliberately to seek sexual pleasure apart from marriage is gravely sinful. It is not uncommon to find that even "French kissing" is forbidden as a "serious occasion of sin." In this whole matter, as in the question of adolescent masturbation, most confessors take a rather lenient attitude. If the couple are of marriageable age and are serious about each other, they are usually advised to "keep trying." One has the impression that the official stance here is one of resigned tolerance of an unavoidable bad thing. But this is not a satisfactory solution practically or theoretically. Most couples feel justifiably more sinned against than sinning when their honest efforts at expressing the kind of love they feel for each other is interpreted as some kind of furtive wrongdoing. How does a couple manage to work for a continuous development of a marital kind of love (spiritual, emotional, *and physical*) if sexual intercourse is expected of them on their honeymoon, but not even a sexual touch is permitted before that? Moralists have traditionally allowed greater liberties between engaged couples than for couples with no intentions of marrying, but the extent of these liberties is rather vague and does not include sexual acts of any kind.

LEVELS OF SEXUAL EXPRESSION

To answer this, it is necessary that we distinguish at least four different types of chastity: the chastity of the married state, of the engaged state, of the single dating state, and of the celibate religious life. The traditional moral thinking accepts two: the chastity of the married life and the chastity of the single (celibate) life. There are profound differences, first of all, between the chastity of the individual who has chosen the celibate life as part of his vocation and the single person who is not yet married, but either intends to or has not ruled it out completely. The day-to-day problems, the attitudes, defenses, and values, the conflicts, frustrations and tensions, and the long-range orientation that provides the structure for sexual morality will all differ significantly. Similarly, the married state differs in an obvious manner from the single and the celibate. Our concern here first is with the single, as yet uncommitted person. The rules of chastity which apply in this case must be differentiated from the rules of the married and particularly of the celibate life. In addition, we feel a fourth distinction is necessary: the chastity of an engaged couple, which will be discussed later.

A single person who is of dating age but not yet engaged to marry should be in the process of developing relationships with a number of persons of the opposite sex. Gradually there is built up a more or less conscious standard for choosing a marriage partner against which other persons are measured. The maturation of this standard is dependent upon a certain number of dating relationships. Love is not blind. Mature love depends upon a fairly conscious assessment of the loved one. This evaluation can be valid and mature only when a person has, through several relationships, developed and defined a hierarchy of qualities that are necessary and desirable in a potential spouse. Because the physical attraction of the other is an important component of marriage, these relationships demand some physical contact such as hand-holding, dancing, kissing, and limited necking.

The limits of affectionate and sexual expression should be defined primarily in terms of the young man, since sexual arousal in women is more diffuse and emotional. A pattern of actions which regularly evokes an erection in the man is morally questionable. This is so because once an erection occurs in this context, the entire person is sexually aroused, and the direction of activity focuses on genital gratification. Emotional preoccupation very quickly takes over control of judgment. That is, once a couple realizes that their affectionate activities have reached a level at which the man is physically aroused, they are beyond the level of mere affectionate expression. This does not mean that if a couple inadvertently go beyond this, they have committed a grave sin. But it does mean that their behavior in the future must reflect a recognition of the danger.

If there is a genuine attempt to change the tactics or the situation, then the moral orientation is operating well. If not, then they realize that a potentially serious habit is developing. This general principle allows for physical contact and intimacy, yet seeks to avoid exploitation which can be rationalized as "getting to know one another." This broad rule also allows for a sexual-moral orientation rather than a self-conscious, act-specific morality. If on occasion a young man is sexually aroused, he need not feel that this is seriously sinful. His responsibility lies in changing the situation so that he does not fall into a pattern of overt sexual gratification. Human nature is such that an individual or couple cannot for long control sexual arousal at a level of partial gratification. Sexual arousal creates increasing tension that pushes toward complete gratification.

It has been a common mistake to place the greater part of the burden of premarital prudence upon the woman. The attitude often has been that the woman must set the limits of physical intimacy. This results in two problems. First, the woman is generally much slower to sexual arousal and consequently may not accurately distinguish affection from passion. Second, there is an implicit, if unintended, reduction in the young man's responsibility. The period of free dating must have sexual restraints. Without them, it is too easy to confuse passion with permanence, infatuation with commitment. Unless the person has developed a realistic and mature set of expectations for a potential spouse, there is too much emotional preoccupation in a sexual relationship to allow deliberation. A premature sexual relationship can short-circuit the more mature but more difficult development of a relationship in all its aspects.

The mutual decision of a couple to commit themselves to each other permanently, based on a dating relationship that has allowed a high degree of acquaintance with the total personality of the other, necessitates a fourth kind of chastity. Engagement is a mature, thought out decision, the result of a relationship that has strengthened and deepened between two mature persons. Because this relationship demands greater intimacy, it also demands greater maturity than the previous level of dating. The engaged couple now claim exclusiveness, commit themselves to permanence, and are preparing for the possessiveness of marriage. Traditionally, moral theology has recognized this by allowing an engaged couple greater intimacy or, more negatively, to put themselves in the proximate occasion of sin because the reason is sound.

Several goals must be achieved during this interval before marriage. One is the gradual unlearning of defenses and inhibitions built up over several years in the area of sexual attitudes and behavior. It is critical at this time that the couple abandon a "do not touch" attitude that may have served to control impulses in the past. For some persons, the reduction of anxiety over expression of sexual feelings is facilitated by the prohibition against intercourse. That is, the couple can become aware of their differing rate of sexual arousal without the threat of having to demonstrate complete sexual competence. This gradual learning will do much to increase their chance of early sexual adjustment in marriage. This goal cannot be achieved, however, if the individuals are still trying to live up to a kind of sexual control appropriate to the single life. Physical intimacies must be seen not as a tolerated weakness, but as a psychologically and morally necessary preparation for marriage.

A second goal to be achieved during this time is the integration of the sexual and the personal-affectionate aspects of love. This entails the overcoming of an essentially adolescent separation of sexual drives from the idealized love object. Prior to the achievement of this integration, many young men and women put the loved one on a pedestal—a carry-over of the mother or father image—and suppress sexual impulses toward this person. If the individual happens to have many "good" qualities, this often reinforces the separation. This attitude has its origin in part in moral training which sets up a dichotomy between good behavior or good individuals and sexual behavior or bad individuals. It is during the time immediately preceding marriage that this incorrect attitude must be replaced by a conviction that sexuality is an integral part of a love relationship.

There is no such thing as a platonic relationship between a single man and woman who are dating. Denial of the role or strength of sexual impulses can only lead to a tentative, defensive relationship. This necessary integration cannot be achieved in a context of modesty appropriate for the celibate life. It needs reinforcement through demonstration that the idealized love object is indeed capable of expressing sexual feelings and that these feelings flow from love for the other person. Maturity of psychosexual development is achieved when this integration of the personal-affectionate and the sexual aspects of love occurs. Its achievement is facilitated when the other responds in a similar way, both sexually and personal-affectionately. If a "do not touch" attitude persists during the engagement period, there is going to be an even more difficult sexual adjustment to be made after marriage. Because engagement is the transition stage from the single to the married state, the arousal of strong sexual impulses is a necessary learning experience for the couple. Their knowledge of each other must increase progressively through experience during this time. It would be unreal to exclude the sexual area from this greater knowledge, as this dimension is central to the relationship.

This leads to a third major goal of the engagement period, that of establishing free communication. In the sexual area, a couple needs to discuss all aspects of their current and future sexual relationship. This is as necessary as a discussion concerning money, home, relations with in-laws, or any major factor in marital adjustment. Two young people cannot assume that because sex has been called an instinct, its expression and gratification are automatically provided for by nature. Fears, anxieties, inhibitions, shame, and embarrassment concerning sexuality cannot be resolved by ignoring them. An individual should know his future spouse's physical and emotional sensitivities and vulnerabilities in such things as nudity and foreplay. Each needs to understand the other's degree of spontaneity, amount of reserve, and ability to enjoy pleasure. All these attitudes and more are communicable if the couple makes a point of talking about sexuality. No one can *assume* that his or her future spouse knows or feels the same way about anything. Such basic facts as the difference in rate of arousal between men and women, frequency of orgasm in women, or difference in response to various kinds of erotic stimulation are not known by most young adults.

If a couple is to grow in their love and knowledge of each other, gradually overcome their inhibitions and embarrassments, and communicate effectively with each other, they cannot be constrained by rules that apply to the single, uncommitted, or celibate life. These goals cannot be achieved in an atmosphere of guilt or uncertainty. The engaged couple must develop an increasing sense of freedom with a simultaneous awareness of the real restraints. This is merely a rewording of what has been described as a mature moral orientation. A couple knows when their actions are directed more at orgasm than the expression of affection, overcoming of embarrassment, or increasing their knowledge and love. In the former case, there will be a disproportionate emphasis upon the sexual dimension of the relationship. More attention will be given to arranging situations such that there is a maximum of seclusion and sexual stimulation. In the latter case, the couple recognizes that certain actions are more arousing than others, and both make an effort to limit gratification to actions that are not just shy of intercourse. It must be mentioned here that an engaged couple who have intercourse because they went too far in expressing affection, without setting up the situation or deliberately planning it, are not guilty of serious sin. Their obligation is to resist the impulse to repeat it and to avoid duplicating the situation that led to it. This demonstration *of ability to tolerate tension and frustration is a critical part of proving fidelity.*

There is bound to be dissatisfaction with some statements in this chapter. Vague general principles and an emphasis upon an amorphous construct such as moral orientation are unsatisfactory to many who seek specific ordinances governing specific behavior, either as confessors, counselors, or teachers, and as individuals grappling with this very problem. Many feel that to trust in the individual's intention or orientation is to throw open the gates to moral relativism or situation ethics. We feel that, on the contrary, moral decisions and behavior that result from an orientation rather than judgments of discrete acts are immeasurably more mature and responsible. Even in as difficult an area as premarital sexuality, this will result in more truly moral behavior in the future.

NOTES TO CHAPTER SIX

1. N. Cameron, *Personality Development and Psychopathology* (Boston: Houghton Mifflin, 1963), 659-671.

2. W. Ehrmann, *Premarital Dating Behavior* (New York: Holt, 1959); A. C. Kinsey, W. B. Pomeroy, and C. E. Martin, *Sexual Behavior in the Human Male* (Philadelphia: Saunders, 1948); A. C. Kinsey, W. B. Pomeroy, C. E. Martin and P. H. Gebhard, *Sexual Behavior in the Human Female* (Philadelphia: Saunders, 1953).

3. St. Thomas Aquinas, *Summa Theologiae*, II-II, Q. CLIV, art. 2, (in corp.); (Rome: Marietti, 1948).

4. G. P. Murdock, *Social Structure* (New York: Macmillan, 1949); C. S. Ford and F. A. Beach, *Patterns of Sexual Behavior* (New York: Harper, 1951).

5. Kinsey, *op. cit.* (1953), Ch. 9; J. T. Landis, "Length of Time Required to Achieve Adjustment in Marriage," *American Sociological Review*, XI (1946), 666-677.

6. Cameron, *op. cit.*; R. R. Sears, E. E. Maccoby, and H. Levin, *Patterns of Child Rearing* (Evanston, Ill.: Row, Peterson, 1957); S. Freud, *The Ego and the Mechanisms of Defense* (London: Hogarth, 1937).

7. Cameron, *op. cit.*, 127.

8. Kinsey, *op. cit.*, 1953.

9. Landis, *op. cit.*

10. J. Bernard, "The Adjustments of Married Mates," in H. T. Christensen (ed.), *Handbook of Marriage and the Family* (Chicago: Rand McNally, 1964), 675-738.

11. H. Benjamin and R. E. L. Masters, *Prostitution and Morality* (New York: Julian Press, 1964).

EPILOGUE

MANY WHO HAVE FOLLOWED US to the end of the arguments in the preceding chapters will be deeply disturbed for two apparently contradictory reasons. On one hand the book seems far too radical. It goes against all kinds of notions we have heard, believed, and perhaps taught most of our lives. "Conservatives" will be upset, perhaps even scandalized, by this challenging of "what the Church teaches" in matters as obviously important as the age of reason, mortal sin, and sexual conduct. On the other hand, "liberals" will be impatient with what must seem to them as rather ludicrous attempts to be faithful to certain principles and ideas of a philosophical tradition which is quite obviously dead and best left buried. Others, more middle-of-the-road, will be annoyed at the attempt to establish sweeping conclusions on such apparently fragile evidence.

In a remarkable little book, *The Changing Nature of Man*, Professor Hendrik Van den Berg talks about the rise of modern psychology and its attempts to reflect upon and somehow deal with the questions: Does human nature change? Why was psychology so long in coming? Having been born, why does it no longer confront the questions that seemed so basic thirty years ago?

> Did people in the nineteenth century . . . know how to educate their children, how to treat their wives! Did employers know how to handle their employees? Did people know the tricks of the different phases of life and could they recognize the dangers where the one phase changes into the next? Did they know which occupation suited them best? Did no one ever have doubts about being the right man in the right place?

Apparently they did know the answers; for no one asked. At one point people must have begun to ask. It is not clear why or from whom. Certainly they did not learn to ask from the psychologist: the questions were there even before he thought of answering them. What then had happened? What knowledge had been lost, and how?

The secret is: we do not know. . . .

The pychologist's skepticism is caused by an inability from which everyone is suffering, *the inability to build upon the certainties of old* [italics ours]. . . . His science is leading him to an acknowledgement of the fact (which has always been known, but which has been kept a secret) that the gap of not-knowing which divides one person from another, and which divides anybody from his future, cannot be bridged by psychology. He is discovering the *raison d'etre* of his science, he is discovering that psychology is an emergency bridge between two banks which had never been separated before; banks which became banks because the earth which we live on has split apart. The connection between them has disappeared to such an extent that no sage, not even a modern hesitating sage like the psychologist, can repair it with his words or even bridge the gap. That is what the modern psychologist is discovering. The realization of this fact leads to the idea that the emergency bridge called psychology fails because nobody knows how to discover the bridgeheads.

. . . .What is the nature of the relationship between the old and the young? Why does nobody know anymore how to act in this relationship? . . . What has happened to the child, that it does not let itself be caught, that it escapes, that it seeks its own way, often losing it, often wandering, but finally, as if by a miracle, maturing after all? As long as these questions are not answered, every pedagogic advice will remain floating in the air. And finally: what has happened to the relationship between husband and wife? What has made them need the almost unbelievable spate of books on sexology? As long as this question is not answered, every attempt to help solve marital problems will be founded on quicksand.

What has happened to us?[1]

"Today the Church is witnessing a crisis underway within society. While humanity is on the verge of a new era, tasks of immense gravity and amplitude await the Church, as in the most tragic moments of its history." These words of Pope John as he convoked the Second Vatican Council contained the ideas which would later be the almost clichéd hallmark of the Church in our time: *crisis of renewal.*

Our time is indeed a time of unprecedented crisis. Never before have so many problems of such vast importance for the entire world been confronted with so few guidelines from the past. If past changes in society can be compared to a kind of combustion process, it seems that the processes of history today can be called explosive. Various biological and ecological factors have combined to put more people on the globe in the last fifty years than have existed in the last thousand centuries. As if the suffocating problems of sheer numbers of people were not enough, modern technology has triggered enormous socio-economic and political upheavals which can only be called revolutions. For example, the collapse of the British Empire—once the mightiest in world history—happened within the past twenty-five years. Its dissolution was so swift and complete that it has no real parallel in human memory. Furthermore, we are experiencing right now a social revolution which, as Commager says, is itself the greatest revolution in five centuries. Practically instantaneous worldwide communications have brought to birth what Teilhard de Chardin dreamed of: a "noosphere" of collective consciousness, a "quantum leap" in the development of the human mind.

For the first time in history, a "one world" that is based on something more than sheer military or political power is possible. Many people are realizing with deep disquiet the implications of an awful Biblical truth: God has indeed "delivered man into the hands of his own counsel." There are two poles of that mysterious tension which is human existence. Potentially infinite, it is fundamentally contingent. With almost no limit to what he can think of (and apparently whatever can be conceived of can sooner or later be done) man can make Eden bloom again for all men on earth. He can also, by a gesture as trivial as eating a fruit, annihilate his species. Jeremiah's words were never so prophetic: "See, I give you authority over nations and kingdoms, to root up and to pull down, to wreck and to ruin, to build and to plant."

It seems inconceivable that such a profound restructuring of the matrix of human society should not produce fundamental changes in the very way we perceive truth and reality. The learning processes by which a person becomes a member of society involve much more than finding out how to speak, act, perform a job. Socialization is the process by which a human animal becomes a *person*. It causes and shapes the very way we feel, think, respond, and behave. Changes in the society ultimately imply changes in the thinking and feeling patterns of members of that society. If change is moderate and continuous, the individual will hardly be aware of the fact that he is constantly adapting his mental and emotional processes to the changes in his society. If changes are abrupt he will experience difficulties in adaptation which will tend to manifest themselves in increased anxiousness, uncertainty, ambivalence, even erratic behavior, all in proportion to the suddenness and intensity of socio-cultural change.

People over thirty years of age are trying valiantly to adapt to the changes by putting on different eyeglasses. We tend to overlook the fact that younger people have been *born* into this exploding modern world. They do not need new glasses. They have new eyes.

The Second Vatican Council did not inaugurate changes which were pulled out of a hat. To a large extent the Council was an expression in the sphere of institutional religion of a complex of forces acting everywhere in modern life. It would be at best naive to view the Church's teaching authority as a quasi-clairvoyant, almost miraculous discovery of truths and solutions to problems. Nor does the Church hand out revelations as though they were parcels of truth in a divinely perennial grab-bag. Rather, it is the function of the teaching office to authenticate and give institutional expression to the dynamic charisms never totally absent within the Church and which are found in special force and abundance in times of great urgency and need. Perhaps not since Pope Leo the Great envisioned the rise of a new civilization out of the ashes of Rome in the wake of Attila has such comparable courage and vision been so needed by leaders.

The goal of all moral and religious training is the development of a morally mature, responsible adult. There is confusion, however, about the best way to accomplish this. The many recent innovations and changes of emphasis in religious education testify to the depth of the questioning. Maturity in moral matters demands an adult conscience. An adult conscience is one that is free of the magical, act-oriented prohibitions of childhood and has advanced to a level at which the assessment of personal right and wrong is made in terms of one's moral orientation. This conscience is also relatively autonomous, that is, open to the advice and counsel of others, but capable of independent functioning. Personal responsibility means that the person has outgrown dependence upon another or upon an institution to tell right from wrong in moral matters. Others are consultants or advisors, necessary to check the validity and consistency of one's conscience, but the final decision rests within the individual. This fundamental premise of moral theology has not been adequately explained to Christians. Most still feel that they are not responsible or capable to determine the right or wrong of their behavior, but that this can be done only by a priest or minister. In this regard, Monden states:

> One who sets out to ascertain the average ethical level of the ordinary Christian of our times will find little cause for satisfaction. We must honestly admit that the Catholic conscience shows a *frightful amount of infantilism.* Every priest in the ministry continually meets remnants of a half-magical attitude toward guilt and sin, expressions of a legalistic taboo mentality, which have hardly anything to do with a grasp of the Christian calling and the need for salvation. There is more: he constantly notices that this state of mind continues to be promoted, consciously or unconsciously, and presented as the real Christian ethic, by quite a number of parents or educators who consider themselves pious Christians, and even by priests in the ministry.[2]

It is obvious that the attainment of an adult conscience demands developmental modifications in order to prevent fixation at a childish level. That is, with increasing age, the person's values, attitudes, and judgments ought to change accordingly. A code of morality sufficient for early adolescence is totally inadequate for the same person as husband, father, and executive. A child should not see disobedience in the same way at ages eight and twelve, for instance. As his world becomes more peer-oriented, his moral judgments ought also to include more of the social dimension. Parents can, with some difficulty, foster the older child's developing moral autonomy. It necessitates for parents the abandonment of black-and-white judgments and advice about the child's moral questions and behavior. It further demands the gradual reduction in parental certitude that their views are always right. Adolescents have the right to make mistakes in moral judgment just as they will in other areas. Without the chance of some mistakes, there is no real opportunity for learning. Older children and adolescents who are given answers rather than being allowed to discuss problems will retain a dependent moral orientation.

It must be acknowledged at this point that from a personal, parental, or institutional point of view, the authoritarian solution is the easiest. It is far less difficult to tell someone or to be told that an action is right or wrong, permitted or forbidden, than to discuss and analyze all the relevant factors and to insist upon a personal evaluation and decision. Yet without the anguish of some uncertainty, there can be no mature moral responsibility. Protection and direction are for children.

Mature moral freedom entails some anxiety. Only specific rules and commands can be obeyed blindly and without anxiety. When concrete rules are known, the individual does not have to assess the right or wrong. Broad moral principles can never be obeyed blindly or without anxiety, for they demand that the person apply them to his own situation, deciding for himself his motivation and responsibility. In the case of children and members of some religious orders, for example, the specificity and concreteness of the rules do not allow the freedom of self-determination. All that is required is obedience. The specification and application of moral principles to a particular situation can only be achieved by a mature, responsible person, capable of tolerating the anxiety of uncertainty.

Only the person himself can know all the aspects of his situation, can sense the strength of a habit, or can modify his patterns of behavior. Most often, it is true, he needs help to clarify issues or to avoid deceiving himself. The confessor or counselor can fill this role in reality testing. If a person needs someone else to tell him that an action is right or wrong, his moral development has been arrested at a childish level.

In this regard, it is necessary to point out grave contradictions in some "liberal" practices. Obviously, the heavy-handed authoritarianism of the Church in the past is neither applicable nor acceptable today. One reaction by many priests is to adopt what they consider a liberal position on certain contested issues. This takes the form, for example, of allowing use of "the pill." But to tell a couple that they may use the pill is not at all liberal. It is the worst kind of seductive authoritarianism. There is no essential difference between saying "Thou shalt not" and "Thou can go ahead and do it." The result in both cases is an infantilization of the subject. There persists in most persons from their early years a need for structure and direction which give security. Ambiguity and uncertainty cause anxiety; the more important the issue, the more intolerable is this type of anxiety. A person with strong feelings and attitudes about the primacy of moral matters will, as his anxiety mounts, seek ever more desperately for a solution. If a solution is offered from outside, the anxiety is reduced and the problem solved subjectively—and temporarily. But it is solved at the cost of autonomy. The dynamics of this dilemma are thoroughly discussed in Fromm's *Escape from Freedom.*[3]

Perhaps the best example of the conflict between autonomy and dependence is provided by psychotherapy. An individual suffering from anxiety presents himself for "help." In most cases there is an implicit, sometimes overt, wish for the therapist's active intervention. It comes as a distinct letdown to the person when he discovers that the burden of direction is his and that he is the ultimate agent of change.

Authority and its imposed rules can often serve as a mask for problems within the person. As an example, so long as rhythm was the only means open to Catholics who wished to avoid children, it served as a perfect scapegoat for sexual problems in a marriage. However, with the advent and popularity of the pill, it became apparent that many couples were not liberated from oppressive sexual restraints, but rather found themselves confronted by the reality of a sexual problem in their marriage. Paternalistic moral authority can also lead to explicit contradiction, if not implicit blasphemy. Consider, for example, the simultaneous invocation of God's help in a "just war" by the hierarchy of both countries. By the assumption that God is on "our side," the consideration of the morality of the war is taken away from the people.

There are no doubt many who feel that the positions advanced in previous chapters were too traditional, too intent on linking past with present. In all cases, the original evidence was psychological, not theological; its agreement with traditional theological positions was not in order to defend them, but resulted from the fact that good psychology and good morality cannot be in conflict.

In many situations, the application of psychological knowledge results in an apparently conservative position. The best illustration of this is the area of impulse control. Despite opposing theories by writers such as Albert Ellis, the mainstream of thinking in psychology definitely supports the establishment and maintenance of impulse controls. Personal adjustment, interpersonal relationships, and social stability depend upon mastery of impulse. This is not to say that a clear understanding of psychological principles of adjustment would lead to a traditional Catholic moral position, but rather that the two positions complement and reinforce one another. Moral theology alone has become incapable of defending its traditional conclusions. Psychology alone, on the other hand, does not compel one to accept any particular ethical position. But the reasoned conclusions of science can confirm what has always been valid in the teachings of moral theology, although many of these principles were all but buried in derivative, act-oriented legalism.

It is popular to speak of a moral crisis that exists among youth today. The implicit meaning of this is that young people are acting contrary to all moral principle. This is certainly not true. There may perhaps be even more behavior today that is motivated by moral value than in past generations. Consider, for example, the generosity of involvement in such areas as civil rights, peace, and volunteer work. There certainly is a conflict between what has been taught as moral law and what young adults today see as moral principle. They perceive the inadequacies and irrelevancies in an act-oriented morality. They also reject the authority behind that morality.

The search for valid principles *is* the crisis. It is caused in part by two opposing forces. One is a quest for certainty and the other is a rejection of authority. The quest for certainty is natural and is heightened by ambiguity in important areas. But young adults today reject the easy solution of accepting the answers of authority. They feel that the security of this certainty is dehumanizing, therefore unacceptable. They believe that the way in which authority perceives the world is not accurate. It is not their perception. They also see the difference between what authority says is right and what it does.

The separation of these two elements, the need for certainty and rejection of authority, is in part responsible for the cleavage between the conservative-reactionary group and the liberal-radical group. The conservative-reactionary position can be extreme in its pursuit of certainty. As the pressure of uncertainty rises, authority must react with more rigid reliance on the force of tradition and authority. The liberal-radical group can be extreme in its insistence that the acceptance of uncertainty, as a consequence of total freedom, must imply the rejection of authority.

The dichotomy is not a necessary one. There are several avenues to integration. Our approach has been that *authority can be a guide to, not a total cause of, some certainty.* It is as unrealistic to reject all that the past or authority has to offer as it is to depend upon it blindly. In addition, we feel that *an approximation of certainty*, necessarily limited by the individual's own blind spots, *is sufficient for prudent action.*

To return to the issue of impulse control, it is interesting to note that the expression of sexual impulses can be far more easily prescribed by specific rules than can aggressive impulses. There are no moral rules governing the degree of hostility that may be expressed in words, nor the specificity of aggressive fantasies, nor the detailed listing of the proximate occasions of sins of aggression. The problem, therefore, of integrating aggressive impulses into one's moral orientation demands autonomous, responsible judgment even in an externally directed person. The traditional rules of sexual conduct can be obeyed, albeit at some price, because they are specific. There are no comparable norms for aggression. The problems of racial animosity, war, business competition, and even normal, unavoidable interpersonal hostility pose greater problems in moral responsibility than does sexuality. In a later book, we intend to discuss the problem of aggression and moral responsibility.

It is our hope that this book has provoked more questions than it has provided answers. There are no easy solutions to the problems presented. The application of a theological-psychological point of view to moral issues may, however, reduce uncertainty in some areas and, where necessary, create some in other areas.

NOTES TO EPILOGUE

1. J. H. Van den Berg, *The Changing Nature of Man* (New York: Dell, 1964), 13-19.

2. L. Monden, *Sin, Liberty and Law* (New York: Sheed and Ward, 1965), 112.

3. E. Fromm, *Escape from Freedom* (New York: Rinehart, 1941).